CHIVALRY
THY NAME IS
BUBBA

by

ROBIN TRAYWICK WILLIAMS

i

Chivalry ~ Thy Name is Bubba
2nd Edition

@ Copyright 2010 by Robin Traywick Williams
Crozier, VA 23039

Cataloging-in-publication data for this book is available from
The Library of Congress.
ISBN: 978-0-9827019-3-5

Robin Traywick Williams
Author

For information write:

Dementi Milestone Publishing, Inc.
Manakin-Sabot, VA 23103
Dementi@aol.com
www.dementimilestonepublishing.com

Cover design by Tucker Conley
tuckerriver@va.metrocast.net

Manuscript design by Jayne Hushen
jehushen@verizon.net
www.HushenDesign.com

Printed in the USA

Other books by Robin Traywick Williams
Bush Hogs and Other Swine

Contents

Foreword

Our 12-acre farm-ette is located on a hill just south of the North Pole Restaurant in the wonderfully still-rural county of Goochland, Virginia. With two stop lights and fewer than 20,000 people, Goochland is bracing for a tidal wave of urban sprawl from Richmond.

From the vantage point of our hill, I have, over the years, surveyed the James River at flood, various activities at James River Correctional Center (the "State Farm"), a one-calf rodeo in our driveway, endless home renovation projects, wrens nesting in the mailbox, bitter winters, dry summers, the challenge of raising children, the strength of family ties, and several runnings of the Great Crozier Dog Races.

I have been privileged to share, through several newspapers, my observations about the joys of life, the ridiculousness of most things we do and the abiding importance of a few of those things. This book is dedicated to my family, all of whom have provided me the greatest happiness in my life and some of whom have been long-suffering participants in these columns.

My especial thanks go to my mother, Flo Crisman Neher Traywick, who, in so many ways, made this book possible.

Most of these columns originally appeared in a fine weekly newspaper, *The Goochland Free Press*, under the heading "Not far from the Pole." My thanks to publisher Robin Lind for giving me the opportunity to write a weekly column.

A few of these columns originally appeared in another fine weekly, *The Goochland Gazette*. Two pieces, "An Open Letter to the Queen" and "The Occasional Great Crozier Dog Races," first appeared in the *Richmond Times-Dispatch* and are reprinted here with permission.

CHAPTER 1

Lessons in Country Living from South of the Pole

The biggest handicap city people have out here is the notion that living in the country is just like living in the city, only you have a bigger yard. I suggest that we institute a course at the community college to teach people how to get along out here in Goochland County. Evidence of taking this course would be required of all new residents.

The course syllabus would look something like this: Living in Goochland: A survey of the basics of country life. Course will cover social customs, wildlife and weather, with one week devoted to hands-on experience with important tools.

First Week: Social Customs/Pickup Trucks. It is not absolutely de rigeuer that you buy a pickup truck when you move to the country, but your neighbors will get tired of loaning you one after awhile. When you do get around to buying a truck, don't think that one of those foreign-made toy trucks will do. This is Ford and Chevy Country. You need a good ol' American-made, full-sized, half- or three-quarter-ton truck with heavy-duty shocks, an eight-foot bed and an eight-cylinder engine. And don't bother with a bed liner to protect it from scratches. You're buying this truck to use, not to cruise.

You've heard that country people are friendlier. That is because of people driving pickups. Once you have a pickup truck, it is incumbent upon you to wave at everyone else in a truck of any sort, including dump trucks, mail trucks, UPS trucks, Virginia Power trucks, old stake-body trucks, Southern States trucks and of course other pickup trucks. Also, after you've been out here for two or three months, you're expected to know all your friends' and neighbors' cars so you can wave at them, too.

We've not talking about serious, hand-flapping waving. The correct salutation involves lifting one or both index fingers from the top of the steering wheel. If, for some reason, you are unable to raise a finger, the permitted alternative is to jerk your head back and salute with your chin.

Second Week: Social Customs/Tractors. Another optional but important piece of equipment for rural residents is a tractor.

Buying and owning a tractor will do wonders for your assimilation into the community. You will endear yourself to longtime residents by asking their advice on your purchase, and you'll meet lots of locals at the auctions where you'll be looking for an 8N tractor with less than 5,000 hours on it. Note: Only city dudes buy new tractors.

Then, once you have your tractor and blade or front-end loader, you'll ingratiate yourself by taking your turn at scraping the snow out of the neighbors' driveways. Note: No one asks for this favor in the country. It is understood that people with tractors will help out their neighbors.

Third Week: Social Customs/Chain Saws. Buying a pickup truck or a tractor might be optional, but buying a chain saw is not. You don't have to buy one with an 8.5-liter engine and a 48-inch bow blade for cutting giant redwoods, but don't buy one that comes with an extension cord. The main thing here is to have a chain saw so you don't have to ask your neighbor for his.

Goochland neighbors are very generous, but nobody likes to loan his chain saw. As sure as shooting, you'll run it through something with a nail embedded in it and your neighbor will be saying unprintable things about city folks again just when you had him convinced you were all right.

Fourth Week: Social Customs/Country Music. It is not necessary to love Loretta Lynn. Taylor Swift will do.

Fifth Week: Meteorology. Learn the difference between "good weather" (rain) and "bad weather" (hot sunny days). A prolonged drought (is there any other kind?) might be great for your suntan, but it is hell for your neighbors, who are interested in raising hay, corn, soybeans, okra, etc. Note: "Bad weather" becomes "good weather" in June when it's time to cut hay.

Sixth Week: Wildlife/Ornithology. A brief look at birds of local interest. All birds larger than a robin are not hawks. Learn to tell the difference between a turkey buzzard, which has a six-foot wingspan and usually soars with others, and a red-tailed hawk, which has a two-foot wingspan and soars alone. (Students who are unable to distinguish the two must learn to bite their tongues before saying, "I saw the biggest hawk today.")

Learn how many bluebird boxes and purple martin hotels you need on your property.

Seventh Week: Wildlife/Herpetology. Although it might be prudent to assume so when it comes to personal encounters, all snakes are not poisonous. Sammy No-shoulders who lives in your garage or under your house is likely to be a beneficial black rat snake. Don't kill black snakes. You will learn in this segment that copperheads are plentiful and poisonous. Leave them alone.

Eighth Week: Current Events. The weekly newspaper is a basic tool for understanding life in the country and you should read it.

However, if you really want to know what's going on in your community, you have to allocate at least 30 minutes a day to hanging around "the store." "The store" can be Wood's Store in Sandy Hook or Whitney's Store in Oilville or any of the other such establishments in the county.

News of neighborhood goings-on used to be swapped by men in overalls around the cracker barrel until the Food and Drug Administration said you had to hang a Plexiglas tent roof over it and put tongs on the side for fishing out crackers and the store owners said forget it. Now folks hang around the video carousel or the self-serve microwave oven and discuss the rabid 'coon Jonna Barber's dogs found or the leaf fire that got away from Sherry Sackett or the good cutting of alfalfa Mike Harris made.

The peak news hours at "the store" are 7 a.m. to 9 a.m., when people are getting their mail and their morning coffee, and lunchtime, when people are picking up a can of viennas (pronounced vy-EE-nas) to go with their chili dogs or sloppy joes.

The location of "the store" sometimes changes over the years. For instance, Taylor's Country Store (Crozier Foodland) only became "the store" after two transactions occurred in the commercial district of Crozier. First, Harvey Layne sold the North Pole Confectionery to Dick Rossi, and second, Bill Towler sold Crozier Foodland to Georgia Rae Roberts.

Ever since the late 1920s, the North Pole had been "the store" in

Crozier. Harvey Layne ran it as a breakfast and lunch place -- and also an appliance store and insurance office. You could even buy a few groceries or one of Phyllis Layne's fabulous pies out of the display case, and you could find out all the news by sitting at the counter and seeing who came in.

Sometimes you had to hang around two or three hours to see everybody and get all the news.

Folks in Goochland love to tell the story about Richard S. Reynolds and the North Pole. It hasn't been told in print in a long time, and we've already established that thousands of new people have swelled the population here, so it is probably time to tell it again. I've heard numerous versions, all of them from people swearing to know, first-hand, The Way It Really Happened. This is my favorite:

Reynolds was spending a few days at Little Hawk, his horse farm on Cardwell Road, while one of his underlings at Reynolds Metals was in Europe trying to negotiate some deal. Reynolds had told the man if he hit a snag to call him at the farm.

Sure enough, the man decided he needed to consult with the boss. This was back in the days before direct dialing, and the man had to place the call through the overseas operator. The phone rang in the barn, however, and one of the grooms answered. As the man in Europe listened anxiously, the operator said, "I have a call for Richard Reynolds."

And the groom said, "He ain't here. He's gone to the North Pole."

There was a stunned silence in Europe before the man gasped to the operator, "Find out when he'll be back."

So the operator asked how long Mr. Reynolds would be gone, and the groom, ever helpful, said, "When Mr. Reynolds goes to the North Pole, he generally stays all afternoon."

Dick Rossi bought the North Pole in 1979, enlarged it and turned it into a delightful pub. However, since it wasn't open for breakfast or lunch anymore, the North Pole ceased to be "the store."

Bill Towler is a big, gentle bear of a man who must have made a living selling beer and soft drinks, because, aside from the contents of the beverage cooler and the jar of pickled eggs, Crozier Foodland appeared to have the original inventory it came with when Towler began operating the store in his youth.

Towler has a hearty voice and always boomed out, "Good morning, neighbor," whenever anybody came in the store. He liked to chat with customers and invariably teased them when he rang up the sale. If the tab came to $1.37, he would say, "That'll be one hundred and thirty-seven dollars, please." It startled me every time, which I guess is why he kept doing it.

When Mrs. Roberts bought Crozier Foodland, she replaced the inventory and opened the store for long hours every day but Christmas. She put in Slim Jims, a coffee machine, and a crockpot of chili to complement the sales of cigarettes, beer, wine and soft drinks.

And before you could say "Richard Reynolds," folks in Crozier were hanging around "the store" all afternoon again.

CHAPTER 2

Blame the Bleeding Liberals

People who move to Virginia from monoclimatic places like Florida or Alaska say one of the things they love about Virginia is the change of seasons. We are blessed with four interesting seasons, which is lucky, because it takes most people every day of summer, fall, winter and spring to recover from Virginia's fifth season: drought season.

We had a cold-weather drought in 1984-1985, but the drought season usually falls in early summer, right before hurricane season and right after you plant 450 azaleas on the bank just out of hose reach.

It's easy to tell when drought season arrives. The rain stops and the temperature is 99 degrees every day for 75 or 80 days in a row. Then a cold front comes through, dropping a fine mist on your neighbor's yard and bringing the temperature down to 94 degrees for 15 minutes.

As natural disasters go, droughts are at the bottom of my list. I'll take floods and hurricanes any day. Floods and hurricanes provide an interesting diversion for about a week --three days of anticipation, one day of actual disaster and three days of cleanup -- and then they're gone. Floods and hurricanes boost morale by giving people the opportunity to be heroic and civic-minded.

But droughts have nothing to recommend them. For one thing, you never get any advance warning. They just latch onto your lawn while you're at the beach and gradually suck all the moisture and life out of everything. And they take too long. It's hard to maintain your enthusiasm for a natural disaster that hangs around for weeks like a smoker's cough.

Plus the spectator factor is virtually absent. You just don't see people driving slowly through the neighborhood taking photographs of parched lawns. Nobody comes out to the country to gasp over fields of alfalfa shedding their desiccated leaves. Financial losses from a drought might be comparable to those from a flood, but 150 acres of roasted soybeans just don't have the visual impact of the James River flowing through a hotel lobby.

No matter how severe they are, droughts are boring. There are no thrilling stories about people climbing trees to escape the drought. Have you ever tried to make small talk about a drought? "Remember the time the Bermuda High got stuck over Emporia and it bounced all the thunderclouds away for two months? Wow! What a time that was!"

Droughts don't inspire bumper sticker philosophers or give anyone anything to brag about ("I Survived the Drought").

Furthermore, droughts haven't the least bit of glamour about them. Floods and hurricanes bring out neighborly concern, volunteer brigades and governmental disaster aid. With a drought, you have to bring out your own hose and operate it yourself. This is perhaps my biggest gripe against droughts.

I've spent every summer since we got married watering bushes. This has led me to conclude that Job couldn't be considered a paragon of patience until he'd dealt with a garden hose. I'm telling you, hoses are the bane of Mankind. They look like such simple devices -- but a more cunning instrument of torture was never invented.

To start with, you never have enough hose. All the hoses in the world laid end to end will not reach from your spigot to the boxwood out front that is getting brown around the gills. And even if they did, the ends would be dented so you couldn't screw them all together.

One year when April stretched into a drought, I bought four new, 100-foot, five-eighths-inch ID, double-ply, triple-option, dual-belted steel radial hoses. They weigh a thousand pounds apiece. Every summer I spend weeks dragging 10 tons of hose around the place.

Of course, before you get a hose where you want it, it hangs up at the other end and you have to walk back to the beginning to straighten it out. Then you walk back to the end to put it under the bush (which is prostrate and panting by now). Then you walk back to the spigot to turn it on. Then you walk back to the bush to see if it's on fast enough. It's not on at all because there's a kink back at the beginning, so you walk back to the beginning to fix the kink.

Then you walk back to the bush to see if it's on fast enough now. It's not, so you walk back to the spigot and give it a quarter of a turn. Then you walk back to the bush.

After several trips back and forth and several quarter-turns, you get disgusted and give it a half-turn. Whereupon the hose belches and spurts water in a high pressure stream which blasts all the mulch and three inches of topsoil from around the bush.

Hose reels are almost as bad as hoses themselves. They are not made for more than one 25-foot hose. When you unreel them, they turn over and the handle digs into the ground 15 times per hose.

Reeling up the hose is worse. No one is strong enough to turn the crank and reel in 10 tons of hose, so you have to carry the hose back to the reel, where it gets all tangled. Then you have to guide the hose onto the reel with your knees to keep it going back and forth in even rows or it will pile up any old way and then you'll have 25 feet left over that won't fit. Of course, as you guide the hose with your knees, you wipe all the mud and dirt off on your pants leg (or skin, as the case may be).

Next time we have a drought, I'm going to move into the city where they won't let you water anything.

The problem is, it's gotten so that we have a drought every summer, and every summer I have to run the hose around the clock for weeks at a time, trying to save a few bushes. And every hour when I go out to move the hose to the next bush, I curse the bleeding liberals for causing me to spend my summers this way.

If it seems like the summers are getting hotter and longer, it's not your imagination. Four out of the five hottest years on record came in the 1980s, and 1988, if it continues at the same pace, will become the new number one sizzler. (--Which it did, at least until it was overtaken by 1998, then 2005 and now 2010.)

Meteorologists say the earth is heating up because of the "greenhouse effect," which is created when people produce large clouds of carbon dioxide from burning coal and oil. All the carbon dioxide from coal- and oil-fired power plants (which is most of the power plants in the world) is forming a sort of greenhouse roof in the upper atmosphere, letting heat from the sun come in but not letting it escape.

This is just the sort of issue you'd expect bleeding liberals to take up with a vengeance. You'd think they'd be out there demanding that fossil-fuel plants be replaced with nuclear power plants, which produce vast amounts of clean energy. But noooo. They are out there fighting --successfully --the construction of nuclear power plants, thereby ensuring that each year will be hotter and drier than the one before.

The bleeding liberals are so anxious to avoid flash-frying in a nuclear holocaust that they are going to turn us all into dried fruit for some celestial trail mix.

Fortunately, I won't have worry about either outcome, because if I have to fool with these hoses much longer, I'm going to commit hara-kiri.

CHAPTER 3

On the Lam

According to Warden John Taylor, the recent search for escaped killer Millard M. Curry was focused on our lower barn on Lee Road...for about five minutes.

"That's as long as it took to determine that Curry had not been anywhere near there," said Taylor.

I was so hoping to lead this column with the information that Curry had spent the night in our lower barn, thereby arrogating to the Williams family a bit of the notoriety surrounding this whole incident.

I was not alone in wanting to be part of this story. Curry's escape and the subsequent manhunt were the hot topic of conversation, not only in Goochland, but the entire Richmond metropolitan area that week, displacing such staples as West Creek, Route 288 and the daily drug-related murder.

It must have been a slow news day because the news media covered Curry's escape only slightly less thoroughly than the death-row escape from Mecklenburg of the infamous Briley brothers and Lem Tuggle.

Warden Taylor seemed mildly miffed at the attention paid to Curry's escape. He thinks the news reporters are missing the big story. "In 1973-1974, we had more than 500 escapes statewide with an inmate population of about 6,000. In 1986-1987, we had 38 escapes with a population of 11,000," he said.

The few escapes from the State Farm generate more excitement in town than out here in the county where the escapee is presumably still hiding. This is largely because of the news coverage, which is produced by people who don't understand the situation around here.

Most news accounts somehow leave you with the impression that the escapee is a bloodthirsty maniac with a Bowie knife in his teeth and an Uzi in each hand, blasting and slashing his way to freedom through a wall of hapless guards and helpless bystanders, and that the escape itself is a well-planned venture that the convict has been preparing to execute for the last 17 years.

With this terrifying picture subtly implanted in people's consciousness, town folks think we country folks are either incredibly cool or incredibly dumb to take such incidents with the aplomb of Eula Duncan. During a 10-second sound bite on WXEX-Channel 8 a few hours before Curry was recaptured, Eula said she wasn't worried and she didn't think many people were, that we had all gotten used to this sort of thing.

What Eula Duncan knows that townies and reporters don't know is that there is little history of risk associated with the escapes from the State Farm. Escapes from the State Farm are nearly always spontaneous and concluded within 48 hours.

The State Farm is, of course, a special case. It is unique among the correctional facilities in the state in that it is a medium and minimum security facility, and the inmates there are generally on their way out of the system. They are either approaching their release dates or appear to be good candidates for parole and have proven themselves not to be escape risks.

According to Warden Taylor, these men are driven to escape by some personal crisis -- a sick mother, a disaffected girlfriend, a threatening fellow inmate.

"We'll always have escapes. We can't control the wife who says 'I don't love you and I'm not going to see you any more.' We can't control the inmate who threatens another for not repaying a loan. We can't control these factors and we can't control how the men react to them."

The escapees are easily caught because they have no plan. Curry, for instance, never left the adjoining property and was captured the second night as he was climbing a fence along Route 6. "They sit under a tree all night, thinking about what they've done, and they realize they've messed up," said Taylor. "Most of them offer no resistance."

I've lived next to the State Farm for 30 years. Although we take certain precautions when we know there's been an escape, obviously the fear of danger from convicts next door has not driven us away from the area. We think, in fact, that the State Farm is a good neighbor.

When I first moved here, I was a little uneasy about living alone near a prison, particularly the first time I turned into Lee Road at night and saw a guard standing in the road with a pump shotgun on his hip. I stopped and rolled the window down about three inches. "What's the matter?" I asked nervously.

He rolled the tobacco around in his mouth and said, "Aw, we got one out."

The neighbors reassured me, advising me to leave the keys in my car and lock the house whenever there was an escape. John Taylor said he heard a variation of that advice from a woman in Rockville who said she not only left the keys in the car, she left a fifty dollar bill on the dash.

The only worrisome incident that I recall involved a State Farm escapee named James Dolan who broke in -- probably sneaked in -- a house in Old Oaks and took a shotgun. Later that same afternoon, Dolan used the shotgun to get the better of the Powhatan Correctional Center warden, whom we shall spare further embarrassment from being named, yet again, in connection with this incident.

The warden drove down a secluded road looking for Dolan and found him. Dolan popped up from behind a woodpile with the shotgun and demanded the warden hand over his truck and his breeches. As Dolan took off for Virginia Beach, the warden headed for a nearby house and a lifetime of ribbing.

It wasn't fun, but at least nobody got hurt.

Sam Callahan, a semi retired employee of Sabot Hill Farm, had a lot better luck in his encounter with an escapee back around 1970.

In those days, the grass airstrip at Sabot Hill was in use, and the Reeds kept an old car with the key in it parked nearby, just in case friends flew in and needed transportation to the house. The car was a weathered '56 Chevrolet station wagon with "Sabot Hill International Airport" emblazoned on the door.

As Stuart Johnson tells the story, the convict had escaped during cool weather and he took shelter in the station wagon. Meanwhile, Sam

Callahan was going about the farm, keeping an eye peeled for the escapee. When he saw a stranger in the station wagon, he went up to him and asked, "Are you from the State Farm?"

The convict said he was.

"They're looking for you," Sam said.

"Yeah, I know," the convict replied.

"Come on," said Sam in the best John Wayne style, "I'm taking you in."

So Sam put the escaped convict in his truck and drove around looking for someone to give him to.

I'm not sure State Farm escapees are that docile anymore, but we like to think so.

CHAPTER 4

The Occasional Great Crozier Dog Races

he Occasional Great Crozier Dog Races is one of those events destined for a two 'graph filler in the back pages of the Goochland Gazette. Actually, that would be stretching it. A casual account delivered by the water cooler (does any office still have one?) is probably all the notice the races will get unless I can talk somebody into publishing this.

As you might gather from the title, the OGCDR is a sort of ad hoc affair. We just had the third Occasional Great Crozier Dog Races. They were held about 10 o'clock Saturday night after two hours of preparation and discussion by the race committee, which met for drinks and dinner (mostly drinks) at our house.

Actually, my husband, Cricket, who is the race committee, was having drinks and dinner at our house anyway. Joe Smith, whose dog, Raoul, is the reigning champion, was there, too. Joe's wife was out of town and it seemed like a good time to have the races.

Crozier is a wide place in the road here in Goochland County, about 15 miles outside Richmond. Everybody gets it confused with Crozet, a little bit wider place in the road on the other side of Charlottesville. There are about 20 houses on Lee Road, where we live, and Joe Smith says everybody who lives in them is weird, but in a nice way. Lee Road is a good place to hold the Occasional Great Crozier Dog Races.

This dog racing business all started one Sunday afternoon a few years ago when Joe Smith and my brother Bo got to arguing over whose dog could run faster. After they had a few beers and showed each other the color of their money, we went out to race the dogs.

Raoul is mostly yellow lab and doesn't look fast. But I'd lived on Lee Road several years, and I'd seen Raoul run along the shoulder, not chasing cars, just running with them, and I'd clocked him at 25 miles per hour, so I knew he could run.

Bo's dog, Will, was the stranger who rode into town for the showdown. Will Rogers was a brown dog whose mother evidently shared a dog biscuit with an Airedale one time. He was little but he could fly. The smart money was on the stranger.

There was, as I recall, little discussion of how to make the dogs race. All it took was five people and a pickup truck.

There's a straight, quarter-mile stretch of road between Locust Bend, where Joe was living, and Contention, where I was living. After some arguing, we took the dogs to Contention and lined them up. Joe's wife took Raoul's collar and I held Will's.

Cricket stood by the mailbox at Locust Bend to judge the winner.

Then Bo and Joe got in the pickup truck and took off, both of them hanging out the window hollering at their dogs. "Come on, dog!"

Raoul and Will took off after the truck, their legs a furry blur in the grass on each side of the road. At first, Will seemed to be getting the best of it, and the little brown dog cheerfully crossed the road several times to twit Raoul.

His uppityness cost him the race. Head down, ears flapping in the breeze, Raoul drove straight for his own driveway, nosing Will out at the finish. Bo and Joe managed to stop the pickup truck in time to see the finish and Joe whooped. Chagrined, Bo vowed his dog would take Raoul in a return match.

To give everybody a chance to win his money back from Joe, we had a shorter race for crippled old dogs (since Joe and I each had one) called the Hundred Yard Hobble.

However, Hot Pants and Rally were not quite as keen about racing as the other dogs. As Joe and I stood by the mailbox, shouting ourselves hoarse at the two old gyps, Hot Pants crawled under the pickup truck and Rally sat down to scratch fleas.

The second Occasional Great Crozier Dog Races was held some time after the first. This time we had a couple of kegs and about 100 people.

Some of them even borrowed dogs to bring. Raoul, who likes to fight even more than he likes to run, tried to pick a fight with most of them, and we ended up with dogs tied to every tree in the front yard.

In any case, we never got around to running the dogs. Will had been dognapped in the meantime, and since he wasn't there for the rematch, we declared Raoul the winner of the Contention Quarter-Mile by default.

This last time, for the third go-around, we actually ran the dogs in an experiment with night racing.

I must say I wasn't too crazy about running our young dog down the road after a pickup truck in the middle of the night. Pigtail's got enough bad habits as it is. But when it was clear that Cricket was determined to have the races, I decided the best thing for me to do was go along and drive the pickup truck.

We put Rally, Pigtail and Raoul (who's almost old enough for the Hundred Yard Hobble now) in the back of the truck and drove down Lee Road, rousting people out in their pajamas for the races.

Naturally, we only went to the houses that had lots of dogs, and naturally, there was a terrible ruckus when we drove up with a truck full of dogs. Cricket wouldn't let me drive away until we had another entry for the OGCDR. It worked pretty well. Folks would do anything to get rid of us.

Leaving each house was a routine worthy of the Keystone Cops. We'd let the tailgate down to add the new people and dogs and immediately some of the ones we had in there would jump out. When we finally had a truckload of people and dogs, we drove to Contention.

Jay Carpenter said his dog wouldn't run away from home, so we agreed to start the race at Locust Bend and let Jay's dog run for home.

Raoul would run any direction, and Pigtail didn't know where she was anyway.

The new handlers didn't know what to do, so Cricket, Joe and I all told them at once how it worked. There was lots of shouting and gesturing and barking.

"Stand over here. Now you hold Raoul."

"I can't. Biscuit'll get jealous."

"Well, you hold Raoul."

"All right, now what do we do?"

"Catch that dog! He's slipped his collar!"

"Watch out! Rally's getting out of the truck!"

"Here, Biscuit. Come back, Biscuit."

"Quit biting, Pigtail."

"All right, get in the truck, get in the truck."

"Shut the tailgate. I'm not driving off with the tailgate down."

"It won't shut."

"It shut coming down here."

"Catch that dog! He's slipped his collar!"

In the end, the race went off before the truck did. The driver wouldn't go but 20 miles an hour for fear of running over one of the entries, and Raoul beat the truck. Pigtail trotted off then went back to the starting line to ask for directions. Biscuit dogged the back of the truck while his owner screeched, "Go faster!"

By the time the truck got to the mailbox at Contention, Raoul's yellow coat was a faint wisp far in the distance.

We picked up the dogs and went back and got the folks at the start, then dropped everybody off at home. Raoul responded to his undisputed championship by picking a fight with one of the neighbor's dogs, and there was a lot of barking and hollering before Cricket and Joe broke it up. Neither dog was hurt, but Cricket had to go to the emergency room for a tetanus shot and bandages on three fingers.

All in all, it was something to talk about until the fourth Occasional Great Crozier Dog Races.

Editor's note: The newspaper has learned that the race committee of the OGCDR will be filing an application to have pari-mutuel betting at the next race meet.

CHAPTER 5

Don't Scare the Turkeys!

The contractor who is doing the addition to our house couldn't come over for us to sign the contract last Friday because he was turkey hunting. It is spring gobbler season.

When he came by a couple of days later, I asked him how it went. He said he heard a lot of turkey hunters but no turkeys. He said the turkey hunters were calling turkeys and they made the woods sound like every crow and owl in Virginia was perched in the trees around him.

Every crow and owl? What happened to the championship turkey callers, you know, those long, shallow boxes with a handle you scrape across the edges to make a gobblegobblegobble sound?

You could play those things like a bastardized violin, scraping slowly or passionately, depending on your particular philosophy of turkey calling. In certain parts of the country they even have contests to determine the most talented turkey caller, sort of like hog calling contests, I imagine.

Well, I was stunned to find out that gobblegobble turkey calling has gone out of fashion. The theory nowadays, according to our contractor, is that you attract turkeys by making some extraneous woodland noise, like a crow's call or an owl's hoot. When a rutting turkey raises his voice to tell the crows and owls to pipe down, they're spoiling his mood, then the turkey hunter picks up his championship turkey caller and gives it a couple of seductive scrapes.

I was glad to hear that our contractor, a man I judge to be experienced in these matters, had such poor luck turkey hunting. It confirmed my opinion of turkey hunting, an opinion drawn from extensive research conducted during one long, cold day of turkey hunting: It's my opinion that the last wild turkey killed in Virginia became the entree at The First Thanksgiving feast at Berkeley Plantation in 1619.

The Commonwealth of Virginia promotes the fiction that turkey hunters kill turkeys by outlining bag limits and hunting seasons. The spring gobbler season, for instance, opened April 9 and closes May 14. Hunters are allowed to hunt from one half-hour before sunrise until 11 a.m. The bag limit is one bearded bird per day, two birds per season.

But I have never heard of anyone actually killing a wild turkey. What turkey hunters do is go out in the woods and sit and make crow and owl noises for three or four hours and then they come in and get cleaned up and go to work and talk about turkey hunting.

What turkey hunters talk about is how you have to be quiet when you're turkey hunting or else you'll scare the turkeys. Turkeys, even in rut, are notoriously wary of hunters. They are born with a little device in their beards that is particularly sensitive to the sound of rustling camouflage jackets.

I've never been turkey hunting during spring gobbler season, but I'm sure it's pretty much the same as turkey hunting in the fall season. The only difference is that you are allowed to take birds of either sex in the fall, which raises the expectations of turkey hunters considerably. However, the same number of birds is killed in the fall as the spring --none.

My brother, Bo, took me turkey hunting in November one year. I'm not sure how I happened to go except that I like trying new things and I never miss an opportunity to do something with my big brother. Anyway, he had me come down to his house in West Point the night before so as to be ready to go turkey hunting bright and early.

Of course, the day of The Great Turkey Hunt was the coldest day ever recorded in November in North America, or even December. Most of the cold was concentrated in Bo's house, where I lay awake all night shivering. It was a great relief when the alarm went off at 3:30 a.m. and I could get up and put on my long johns, jeans and down jacket.

We got in Bo's truck and drove off in the dark towards a filling station far away where we were to meet Dalton Brownley, who is a serious turkey hunter. All the way to the filling station, Bo coached me in the fine points of turkey hunting: "You have to be real quiet or you'll scare the turkeys," he told me several times.

We picked up Dalton in the dark and drove to some piece of woods far away in the opposite direction. All the way to the woods, Dalton coached me in the fine points of turkey hunting: "You can't make any noise or you'll scare the turkeys," he told me several times.

After driving a long ways in the dark, we turned off onto a rutted logging road and drove another long ways. The men talked and I sat quietly memorizing the fine points of turkey hunting and hoping there was a kerosene heater at the turkey hunting site.

Finally, we stopped and got out of the truck. We had two dogs with us, which you are allowed to use to hunt turkeys during the fall season, but since one of them was a womanizing Airedale and the other one was a German shepherd, we put them in the cab of the truck.

Then we walked a long way into the woods, where Dalton and Bo selected a tree for us to sit by and hunt turkeys. So at first light we sat down with our backs to the tree, loaded our shotguns and waited.

This was back in the old days, before the crow-and-owl calling theory had become popular, and Dalton commenced the hunt by scraping out a few gobblegobblegobbles with his championship turkey caller. We all listened intently for an answering call but none came.

We sat and sat and I got colder and colder, which was amazing since I was just about petrified when we first arrived. Every time I heard a rustle in the leaves, I'd turn my head and my hair would scratch across the nylon shell of my down jacket, making a noise like fingernails on a blackboard amplified 10,000 times. Naturally, this scared all the turkeys away. So, after three hours of turkey hunting by this tree, punctuated by Dalton's turkey calls and my hair scaring the turkeys, Bo stood up and said, "Well, that's enough for today, I reckon."

Then we walked all the way back to the truck and drove all the way out of the woods and drove all the way back to civilization drinking antifreeze to warm up and had breakfast at some diner and talked about turkey hunting.

I was so glad to have been turkey hunting so I could participate in the conversation.

After we thawed out over breakfast, we decided to take the dogs and go deer hunting, which we did in another piece of woods. That was a little more interesting because we had to run around a lot trying to catch the German shepherd, who was gun-shy. By the time we caught the dog, it was lunchtime, so we went back to the diner and talked about turkey hunting some more.

After lunch, we went over to Dalton's daddy's farm to hunt squirrels, which was better than either turkey or deer hunting because we actually saw some game, and Dalton even fired his shotgun. The coldest day in November in North America turned into a nice warm afternoon, and we all ended up snoozing against stumps until nearly sundown.

By then everybody had to get home after an invigorating day of hunting, so I apologized again for scaring the turkeys. "Don't worry about it," Bo said, "that's one of the best turkey hunts we've ever had."

Gobblegobblegobble.

CHAPTER 6

A Neighborhood of Pyromaniacs

I t's fire season again, that period from March 1 to May 15 when it is unlawful to burn leaves, trash, etc. outdoors before four o'clock.

I have a great fear of fire, largely because we live in a neighborhood of pyromaniacs. All of these people are intelligent, educated people who ought to know better.

Like Sherry Sackett, who works at the American Cancer Society. Sherry was burning some leaves and dead stuff she had raked off her garden one afternoon, when the fire got away from her. She turned on the hose she had laid out and it sprouted little fountains like a soaker hose.

So she called us. We grabbed our hose and raced over, only to find our hose was dry-rotted, too.

Fortunately, we live practically next door to the Crozier Fire Department. Amazingly, although this was the first weekend in March and every normal human being was watching the Atlantic Coast Conference basketball tournament, the volunteer firefighters were there in no time.

The forestry warden, Sam Barkley, was there in no time, too. He and Cricket and I stood by watching the firemen spraying and raking the blackened yard. Cricket asked Sam if he was going to give Sherry a ticket for burning before four o'clock.

Sam said, "Yes, I just gave someone else one. I'll have to give her one, too." Then he shifted the tobacco in his cheek and said, "I'm harder on them when they interrupt my basketball."

Sherry's next door neighbor, Clopton Knibb, the former commonwealth's attorney, was very supportive, went to court with her and so on. And later, when one of the leaf fires Clopton regularly builds in the woods behind his house got out of control, Sherry was very supportive in return.

It wasn't too long after Clopton's fire that Michael Parrish tried to blow up his tool shed. He was ostensibly burning up a pile of limbs and branches he'd picked up out of the yard. The pile had been there awhile and the wood was dried out, ready to burn. Howsomever, Mike sloshed a little gasoline on the pile before flicking a match.

Tom Andrews, who was living next door at the time, had just stepped into the kitchen to mix a drink when he heard a horrific explosion and looked out the window to see flames shooting into the air considerably higher than Mike's house.

Mike was suitably chagrined when the fire department arrived.

Mike's house is even closer to ours than either Clopton's or Sherry's. As I said, I view all these incidents with some alarm. But I have a fire story to tell on myself, too.

One afternoon Lake Andrews was hanging over the fence watching me rake leaves. I made several small piles on the gravel driveway, uncoiled the hose and prepared to light the leaves. Then Lake said in a curious voice, "I thought you said Cricket didn't like for you to burn leaves."

"He doesn't," I responded cheerfully," but he went to Abingdon for the night. If they're all burned and the fire's out when he gets home, he won't say anything. He just hates to drive up and see flames in the driveway."

Lake nodded in understanding.

Well, you know what happened. Cricket saw the smoke clear across the state and raced home to catch me in the act. Lake was still hanging over the fence chatting and watching me tend the fires when Cricket drove in the driveway. But she had disappeared by the time he got out of the car.

You know, come to think of it, all these incidents happened when Lake and Tom Andrews were living here on Lee Road. Now they've moved to the Covington development, which the forestry warden says is the neighborhood he is most worried will have a serious fire. Do you think there's some connection there?

CHAPTER 7

Numbers Have Nothing to Do With It

I hit a deer the other night, a yearling that was killed instantly, and it has depressed me to no end. I worry a lot about killing wild animals. I also worry that taking their habitat will threaten the existence of a herd here, a flock there, until more and more species are extinct.

Deer probably don't need my worrying. They've gotten to be practically like squirrels, just as numerous and living in our back yards, too. The people who figure these things out say we have more deer today than the settlers found here 350 years ago. Last season, hunters killed some 119,000 deer in Virginia, 1,049 in Goochland County. And there seem to be plenty left.

But the deer I hit was an individual. It was a terrified youngster who dodged a truck and dove into my grill. I can see its frightened face in my mind.

Those of us who live among wild animals are aware of them as individuals. And though some of us will hunt them in winter and curse them in our gardens, we will go to extraordinary lengths to keep an individual creature from suffering.

I'm thinking of Sandy Fisher, who rescued a tiny fawn whose leg was severed by a mower in a hay field and who raised the deer until it was strong enough to leap the fence and go back to the wild on its own.

I'm thinking of Julian Keevil and Coleman Perrin, who took a swim in the Harrells' lake January to save a deer which had fallen through the ice.

Julian and Coleman, along with Frank McGee, Mary Lamb Lucas, Polly Bauhan and several others, were hunting the Deep Run Hunt Club hounds on foot because of the snow and ice when they came upon a buck thrashing around in the middle of the lake.

The deer had followed a trail out onto the ice, not realizing that the ice of last week was no longer solid. When the foxhunters found him, the deer was making enormous thrusts out of the water, trying to get back on the ice.

"He was getting his front end up on the ice but he couldn't get his hind end up," Coleman Perrin recalled. "No telling how long he'd been in there. He was real raw underneath his chest and just about exhausted then."

Immediately, the hunters began thinking of ways to save the deer. The ice was too thin to get close to the deer, so first they tried to shoo him in another direction by cracking their whips. That didn't work, so a couple of them went around the lake to get a boat.

In the meantime, Julian Keevil recalled, "People were getting a bit upset about it, so I thought, we'll take care of that. Since it was a sunny day, I thought the only thing to do was strip off and go in and try to get a rope around him."

So, Julian -- and soon Coleman -- went in, trying to break a path through the ice to the deer. "The closer we got, the ice got too thick to break and swim at the same time," Julian said.

By that time, Henry Harrell had come out of his house and was poling through the ice in a boat. The people in the boat were able to get a rope around the deer and pull him to shore.

"When he got close enough to stand and walk himself out, he was so cold he couldn't walk. We dragged him out," Mary Lamb Lucas said. "He was in shock, he couldn't stand up."

Holding the deer's antlers in case he suddenly thrashed around, they half-carried him up the bank.

"Then we took off our jackets and rubbed and rubbed him, trying to bring the warmth back. He acted like he wanted to give up. You know how some animals do when they're caught in a trap...the fear kills them," said Mary Lamb.

The rescuers worked for an hour, until the deer was dry and alert and breathing normally. They made a windbreak with the boat and left him covered with blankets. When Henry Harrell went down to check an hour later, he found only blankets.

"We hope he's out romping around somewhere," said Mary Lamb. "There was no doubt we were going to save him. No one expressed any doubt. We just had to do it."

Julian dismissed his icy swim lightly and Coleman's response was the same. "You had to do something. It was an animal that was caught and you didn't want to let it die."

If there is anything Virginia has more of than deer, it's seagulls. But Michael Babb, presently of North Carolina, formerly of Crozier and Virginia Beach, once saved a seagull for pretty much the same reasons as Julian Keevil and Coleman Perrin went swimming one winter.

Michael Babb is a noted softy when it comes to animals. He's the sort of person who has six dogs because he never could bear to part with any of the puppies he bred to sell. (Of course, Michael didn't discover that he felt that way until he had a customer standing there with check in hand, but that's another story.)

So when one of Michael's huskies found an injured seagull on the beach, Michael caught it and carried it home. "He had been shot and his wing was broken, but he wasn't hurt otherwise," Michael said.

The emergency animal clinic wanted to put the bird down right away, but euthanasia wasn't on Babb's agenda that day.

"So I opted to clean out a room downstairs and make him a place to stay," Michael recalled. "I took him to my personal vet the next day and he operated on him. He inserted a wire in the bone, which, in a bird, is hollow, and taped the wing to his body in a folded position."

Then Michael took the seagull home to recuperate in the front bedroom downstairs. He got a large Styrofoam cooler and filled it with water and minnows. "He'd sit on the side and bob for minnows," Michael said. "After he'd dispensed with all the minnows, he'd use it for recreation. He'd get down in it and wash himself."

Meanwhile, Michael's roommate was not pleased. "His name was Barry Fogelsong and he said, 'Babb, we're not keeping any bird in this house.' He complained about the bird all the time. But one day when he didn't know I was around, I heard him open the door to the bird's room and say, 'What cha doing, buddy?'"

After a couple of weeks, Michael took the bird back to the vet, but the wing wasn't healed. In frustration, Michael tried tossing the bird in the air, hoping he would fly away.

"We operated again and left it on longer the second time. The whole process took all summer. Barry volunteered to take the bird back after the second operation. I couldn't do it. Barry would either get to throw him up in the air and watch him fly away or have him put to sleep."

The second operation was no more successful than the first.

Michael said he spent about $150 on the seagull, adding that the vet had been quite generous. "Plus the bird did major damage to the vet's hand pecking him. No stitches involved, but lots of bleeding."

And then there was the front bedroom. "It was ruined. We scrubbed it and painted it," Michael said. "That was a rental place. Our landlord lived in front of us. She knew about the bird, but we were good tenants: We paid our rent on time and we invited her to our parties."

Ruminating over the experience, Michael said, "I thought you could have a bird's wing fixed. I thought it was senseless that his life would be destroyed."

But there are thousands of seagulls...

"There are thousands of dogs. There are thousands of cats, too, and I care for every one of them. Numbers have nothing to do with it."

CHAPTER 8

Chivalry, Thy Name Is Bubba

Very now and then, it seems, certain people fret and gnash their teeth and declare in great despair that chivalry is dead. This declaration is usually based on the failure of modern men to take off their hats in elevators (how many men outside of Texas wear hats anymore?) or to cast their $600 Harris tweed jackets into the gutters over which women in $300 knots of leather which pass for footgear must step.

This is not the time for me to express my opinion on the price of women's shoes. The point here is that judgment on the life-and-death question of chivalry should be based on relevant observations.

Chivalry is not the display of social graces in a situation where nothing is lost by their omission (and I'm the first to say social graces should be displayed on every appropriate occasion). Chivalry is "courage, honor and a readiness to help the weak and protect women." Performing a chivalrous act means helping someone who needs help, not being polite.

I have privately observed for years that chivalry is not dead and never will be, despite the murderous efforts of the National Organization for Women. NOW has nearly eradicated the laudable impulse men have to help women, but in one respect the movement has failed: Men cannot stand to see a woman with car trouble.

The automobile and its arcane innards are the last bastion of the male ego. In the old days (pre-1975 or so), before fuel injection systems, catalytic converters and electronic ignitions were prevalent, even the most non-mechanical man could look under the hood with confidence. Today, even specialists have trouble with the computerized engines, but no matter. The idea that men "understand" cars is a stereotype that is firmly embedded in the consciousness of all women and most men.

Men perpetuate this image with their chivalrous efforts to help women who have car trouble. Luckily for the men, most of these situations have little to do with the engine. As it happens, flat tires and broken tailpipe hangers have more to do with the preservation of the male ego and the practice of chivalry than any other aspect of life.

A woman changing a tire is perhaps the most moving situation a man can run across. A man will abandon his place in a line five miles long at the entrance to a stadium where a game will be played between his favorite team and its arch rival in order to help a perfectly competent woman mechanic change a tire.

I changed a flat tire on my car once when no man happened to find me. I figured out the puzzle ring that became a jack. I loosened the lugs. I replaced the wheel. I tightened the lugs --so tightly that later the garage mechanic couldn't tighten them any more with the air machine thing that goes wherrt!

I am not destitute when a tire goes flat, but men won't believe it. (Let me say here that I welcome help when I have a flat tire, but I admit to ambivalence when an 87-year-old man asks me to step aside while he wrestles with the wheel.)

Whenever I have a flat, I pull off the road and open the trunk to get the jack. That's usually as far as I get. Next I hear squealing brakes as a man stops and leaps out of his car, demanding that I get out of the way while he changes my tire. I do.

Once I had a flat on the interstate late at night. Before I could even get out to open the trunk, a state trooper pulled up behind me. Troopers aren't supposed to give hands-on help to motorists because it takes them out of circulation. They're supposed to call for help and get on with their patrolling.

When the trooper found out I had a flat, he offered to call a wrecker, but I said, no, thanks, I could change the tire myself. As I opened the trunk, he stood there biting his lip. "Are you sure?" he asked.

I told him I didn't need a wrecker but I would appreciate his waiting while I changed the tire so that the bogeyman wouldn't knock me in the head and throw me in the ditch. He bit his lip some more while I put the jack together. I made two turns with the jack before I heard a pained, animal cry. As I looked up, the anguished trooper grabbed the jack handle and thrust me out of the way.

Engine trouble doesn't excite men as much as a flat tire. With a little conning, though, men will become chivalrous about that, too.

I am a curse on starter motors. My old Pinto (80-some-odd-thousand miles) went through five or six. My old Mustang (130,000) went through at least four. The Mustang was straight drive, which I requested so that whenever the starter went out, I could roll the car, jump start it and get home.

On one of the many occasions when the car wouldn't start, I was parked in a parking deck. It was night and there was no one around. Finally I found some construction supervisors who were checking on the day's work.

First I persuaded them to listen to the car to see if it was the battery or the starter. I was certain it was the starter and knew all I needed was a push, but you don't walk up to strangers and say, "Hey, would you fellows mind pushing my car uphill about 15 feet out of a tight parking space and then downhill so I can jump start it, thereby avoiding a $50 wrecker fee?"

They agreed to listen. They listened and said it was the starter. Then they wanted to look under the hood, which I showed them how to un-latch. Then they wanted a flashlight, which I gave them. Then they wanted to know where the starter was, which I showed them (although I was getting a little worried then). They tried, unsuccessfully, several maneuvers. They wanted to give up. "We're not mechanics," they said apologetically. I thanked them and said I'd go call my husband, who was 30 miles away.

They looked at each other. "Come on, Bubba," said one, "let's just push her and jump start it."

I thought they'd never think of that.

My most recent brush with chivalry involved a broken tailpipe hanger. Just as I got onto the interstate, the tailpipe fell off. Well, mostly off. I limped off at the next exit, got out and peered under the car. I didn't mind driving around in something that sounded like the entire field of the Indy 500 and looked like a Fred Sanford reject, but I couldn't figure out what to do about the tailpipe, which was hanging by a thread.

But lo! Bubba and Slim (their real names) pulled up in a station wagon that was only slightly less decrepit than my car and offered to save me. Bubba immediately scrunched his considerable bulk under the car and asked me to hand him a coat hanger. He was dumbfounded when I said I didn't have one. Apparently my car looked like the kind of car that would have old coat hangers in the back.

I found some plastic string and he said, "How far do you have to go?"

Thirty miles, I said.

"Well, I'll just have to tie 30 miles' worth of knots in it," he said cheerfully.

Now that's chivalry.

CHAPTER 9

Attic Memories

Recently, my parents moved and Momma asked me to contribute to the effort by removing my books and things from the attic. There turned out to be nine cardboard boxes, mostly full of books, that belonged to me. I brought them home and put them in the front hall where they stayed for two or three weeks. A friend dropped by and her two children pounced on the piles of books, most of which were just suited to their ages. I was delighted to lend them an armful, delighted to see children like myself who lived to read. They showed me title after title and asked, "What's this one about?"

I was surprised to find I couldn't remember what some were about. There were books whose titles, whose worn covers were as familiar as my den, as beloved as my dog, but whose plots I couldn't recite. Still, I knew which ones I loved best, and I did my best to sell them on the collie stories of Albert Payson Terhune: "Lad of Sunnybank," "Buff: a Collie," "The Way of a Dog," et al. The 12-year-old girl was reluctant to take a dog book because she was afraid it would be sad. I suppose they are sad, in the way that owning a dear pet is sad, because the relationship is inevitably too short. Terhune wrote in the 1920s and some of his observations of the times are quaint today. For instance, he frequently spoke angrily of the danger to dogs which wandered too close to the highway, where "juggernauts careered along at forty-five miles an hour." But his writings about dogs and their incredible bonds with people are timeless.

We always had dogs, mostly border collies, but once we had a registered show collie of impeccable breeding. His name was Burruss's Red Rusty and he was a magnificent, seven-year- old gentleman when we got him. Rusty was the epitome of all of Terhune's dogs, from the aristocratic bearing and always-immaculate paws to the extreme sense of dignity. Momma got him from our veterinarian, who had been asked by his owner to put him down because he was a convicted chicken-killer. It was a serious charge for a country dog but it turned out to be a bum rap. In the four years that we had him before his death, Rusty never so much as looked cross-eyed at the bantam flock that ran loose in our stable yard.

In looking through the boxes with the children, I was surprised to see how many "Mother West Wind" books I had. I discovered these charming stories of Reddy the fox, Bowser the hound and other animals one year at Peakland Elementary School in Lynchburg, Va. That summer, I read as much of Mother West Wind as Jones Memorial Library had. That brought on several memories:

My old school, one of those solid, square stucco buildings of two and a half stories, was torn down for no apparent reason about 10 years ago. I don't know if anything's been built on the lot or not. My mother's elementary school was torn down for no reason, too. Now they are building a public works project of some kind on the lot. Wouldn't it have made more sense to renovate those school buildings?

Jones Memorial Library, my summer haunt, was closed recently. Fortunately, it is an interesting enough building architecturally to be converted into something else. For most of this century, it was the city's only "public" library, opened by the widow Jones in memory of her husband. It had every book published in the 19th century, as well as a few more recent editions. (When I was writing fiction in graduate school, my professor couldn't understand why I wrote like 19th century authors.) Its stacks were arranged alphabetically by author, a wonderful system that, unfortunately, no one uses any more. You had to hunt around to find books on a particular subject, and the search often yielded something else you never would have thought to look for. The library was on the bus line and I went there sometimes just to browse. It was built like a magnificent home, with marble floors, high ceilings and big windows --grand, but inviting. It was a proper place for books and the people who loved them. You had to be at least 75 to get a job there as a librarian. The librarians all knew me because I often returned books in a picnic basket for my grandmother, who, over the years, read every book in Jones Memorial Library (and saw that I was well started on the same path).

In her will, Mrs. Jones left an endowment, as well as instructions that the library continue under its original charter, which barred blacks. When I was in high school in the mid-1960s, a group of citizens got the city to open a truly public library, complete with all sorts of modernisms like acoustic ceilings, microfiche and the Dewey Decimal System. I went there once.

My husband said he didn't want all those books going up into the attic to mold, but he also got tired of stepping over them in the hall. So I carried them up to the back bedroom, and one night when I had no business staying up late, I began sorting them. I steeled myself to save only the most valuable and to get rid of all those I would never have use for again: my eighth grade American history book, "Our Friend the Cocker Spaniel" (nobody in our family ever had one), a handbook on boomerangs, the 1952 Dun and Bradstreet ratings book for Virginia. (I'm not making this up.)

I think I first realized I was in trouble with this project when I found myself debating over a copy of the 1966 Manual of the Virginia General Assembly. Certainly, I never plan to read it. And its value as a reference book is rather limited. But it is leather-bound, and it does have my daddy's name stamped in gold on the cover. Furthermore, it has a wry nostalgic value. My daddy's name is supposed to be written inside the book as the delegate for the "floater" seat from Lynchburg-Amherst County. He was drafted as a candidate by the Republican party in the days when hardly anybody in the area admitted to such an affiliation. Surprisingly, though, Daddy came up the winner by 15 votes. We all enjoyed his victory for a month or so, until the recount. When the paper ballots had been recounted in the Democratic county, Daddy was the loser by 15 votes. There was great indignation in Lynchburg, and Daddy was drafted to run again the next time. Again it was close and again he lost in the recount. The funny thing is, there are still lots of people who think he won. I'm often asked, "Wasn't your father in the legislature for awhile?" -- Yeah, for about five weeks...

Along the same lines, I had to decide about the 1963 "Flitcraft Compend, Listing Most Prominent Life Insurance Companies." From 1963 to

1968, my daddy sold life insurance. Apparently, he sold a lot of it, because I remember certificates and plaques on his office wall saying "Million Dollar Round Table." Whatever his success might have been, he hated selling insurance. Momma said he came home for lunch every day and she could hardly make him leave afterwards. He still speaks of that period as the darkest of his life. Although he has a wonderful sense of humor, he has never been able to joke about selling insurance. Once, years after he had left insurance, he was going on about how awful it was, and he concluded by saying, "I believe everyone who sells insurance seriously considers suicide at one time or another."

I kept the legislative manual and tossed the insurance book.

Five of the boxes had books that I read and loved as a child. In addition to Terhune's books and Mother West Wind, there were the Black Stallion series, the Tarzan series, Nancy Drew, "Anne of Avonlea," "Misty of Chincoteague" and lots of riding books. Rereading some of my forgotten favorites really slowed me down. I reread an autographed copy of "Roberta E. Lee," Burke Davis's adorable story of the rabbit from Barefoot County who longed to be the most beautiful Southern belle ever. I reread part of Kipling's "Just So Stories." I reread some of Joel Chandler Harris's tales of Brer Rabbit and the briar patch. I reread "The Country Mouse and the City Mouse" and "Little Black Sambo." I never understood why "Little Black Sambo" was declared racist and taken off the market (but I'm sure I'm going to get letters telling me why). It's a precious story about a little boy who is beset by tigers but who gets the last laugh as the tigers run themselves into a puddle of butter. The book ends with Little Black Sambo eating 166 pancakes drenched in tiger-butter.

Another favorite I looked through was Robert Lewis Stephenson's "Nursery Rhymes for Children." I still know one by heart: "The friendly cow all red and white/I love with all my heart./She gives me cream with all her might/To eat with apple tart." For years I thought this poem was composed by Emma Lavinia Victorine Keitt, my grandparents' cook in Cameron, S. C. Emma came to work for my grandparents the day my daddy was born, and she lived in a cottage in the backyard for years after my grandparents died. She had fallen out of a swing when she was a little girl and broken both her legs. Incredibly, they were never set. By the time my grandfather, a doctor, found her, her legs had healed twisted and the child got around by crawling. There wasn't much he could do but give her crutches.

Emma became sort of a legend in our family. Whenever there was a family gathering, the grandchildren ended up in the kitchen listening to Emma. She recited endless streams of poetry, some of it by Stephenson but most of it by her brother, Emanuel Moses Keitt. Emanuel had gone off to the big city (Columbia, S. C.) and, in 1931, published a book called "Poems for All Occasions" (Volume One, Price 50 cents). Emma would accompany her recitations with appropriate gestures and expressions, which ensured that her audience would remember the poems, too.

Poetry recitations notwithstanding, Emma's chief parlor trick was to recite the alphabet backwards, a skill she taught all the Traywick grandchildren. She also gave us sage advice to help us along life's weary way. Most prominent among her admonitions was: "Don't marry a girl 'cause she wear a pretty dress. Look into her background fust or you might get a diworce." As several of us ruefully learned, Emma was right.

Ever since I wrote my first novel, at age six, I've kept journals and boxes of letters, pictures and mementos so that when I'm a dead world famous author, biographers will have no trouble reconstructing my life. It's eerie sometimes to see in the artifacts of youth the prototype of the adult. Besides the usual matchbooks, ticket stubs, show programs and party invitations, I've kept all sorts of little notebooks and compendia of my activities. I was an inveterate list-maker. In every box there were notebooks full of lists: "Name Bands I Have Seen" (I still recognize some of the names), "Boys I Have Dated" (by year and zodiac sign), "Interesting Things I Have Done" (these ranged from walking across a train trestle at night in an evening gown to dating three sets of brothers).

There were also envelopes full of pictures, mostly of people I didn't recognize. It was the same with the lists of people I went out with. You'd think that if you had gotten dressed up and spent a day or an evening with someone, you'd remember the experience. But I kept looking at the lists of names and the photographs and thinking Who are these people? It's mildly horrifying to me to realize that I can't remember every day of my life. I've had such a wonderful life. But I guess I've been so busy having a wonderful life that I haven't had time to practice remembering it all. You have to keep a journal, either written or oral, to remember what happened. Unfortunately, there are huge spans of time about which I remember only highlights: where I lived, where I worked, a couple of special events. What about those afternoons of wonderful conversational exchange at work, in the pub, at a party? Sad to say, they're gone forever.

There was also a list of items from the house I shared with my first husband. It was a list he made for the property settlement to show how things would be divided. I remember how I laughed at the time because he had listed his Eagle Scout certificate -- as if I would contest him for it.

I also found a surprising amount of creative writing from my school-days. In addition to shorts stories and poems, there were numerous outlines and Chapter Ones of novels. One, to be titled "Thunder Rolls," was about a paralyzed orphan girl whose friendship with a horse eventually enables her to walk. The opening line was: "Kim had never known true happiness until she was three." Truly, a long-suffering heroine.

My first novel, "Effie and Beffie," was not in the box, but I think it has survived. I dictated it to Momma when I was six. She typed it single-space and I was crushed when it was only one page long. It was a racy romance about two elephants, Effie and Tarzana, who had escaped from different circuses. (Where else do elephants come from?) When they got married, Tarzana, like a good girl in the '50s, changed her name to something resembling her husband's name, Beffie. However, unlike a good girl in the '50s, Beffie had a baby the day after she got married.

Even my more "mature" writing was funny. I was a great letter-writer, often making rough drafts first. In one of these, written in the instability of the '60s, I harangued a friend not to "float through life like a coelenterate." (I looked that up; it means jellyfish.) In one of the few college papers I saved, I found an analysis of Ellen Glasgow's "Barren Ground." In the section where I was asked whether I liked the book or not, I wrote: "To be frank, it was a depressing book -- and long to boot. Everybody is poor, poor, poor! (Oh, where are the affluent of Henry James?)..."

After some debate, I tossed the notes I took in Ancient History 323 at the University of Virginia. It's hard to believe I ever knew who Tiglath-Pileser II was (or cared), but I knew --and cared -- because of an absolutely hysterical professor named Harry Dell. He was a smallish, 40-ish man with red hair, black cigars and a penchant for outrageous remarks. He taught ancient history as though it were current events, and it worked. His most famous line was "Hubris is a nine-foot marigold." He was the sort of professor whose students would meet him for a beer in the afternoons. I went occasionally, even after I left the university. When I settled in Richmond, I often thought of going back to the Mousetrap for a beer with Harry and the gang. It was nice to know that he was there and, whenever I got time, I could go back and visit. Only one day I picked up the paper and read his obituary. It turned out to be throat cancer.

I decided to keep a few papers from the course. I don't want to forget Harry, and I don't want to forget the lessons I learned.

When the sorting was done, I had eight and a half boxes to put in the attic and 19 books to dispose of. All that sorting for 19 throwaways. Ultimately, I decided it was worth the attic space to save the books and papers I'll never read again, because one day, maybe 25 years from now when we move to a smaller house, I'll again have the pleasure of looking at them --and remembering.

CHAPTER 10

'How We Live in Virginia'
Doesn't Involve Snakes

Telling one kind of snake from another isn't easy from 40 feet away, which is about the minimum safe distance. My daddy says of snakes, "They're all poisonous to me," and that's a good way to think about them, as long as you use that attitude to avoid snakes and not to kill them.

Dr. Charles Blem, professor of herpetology at Virginia Commonwealth University, is one person who can identify snakes at 40 feet--or less. Recently he and his daughter were jogging when somebody shouted at them, "Look out! There's a snake in the road! We think it's a copperhead."

Dr. Blem barely broke stride as he snatched the snake up, eyeballed it and held it out to the gasping observer. "Brown snake," he said and trotted off into the sunset.

Last week, Dr. Blem was canoeing in a tributary of the Appomattox River when he spotted an enormous brown mottled snake sunning itself on a branch. Maneuvering the canoe under the branch, he grabbed the sleeping snake.

The startled snake thrashed around spewing the contents of its scent sac and doing its best to imitate a cottonmouth. Dr. Blem merely made mollifying noises as he pinned the snake and took its temperature with an anal thermometer. Then he popped the indignant snake into a can for later study.

"Jungle Chuck's Snake Show," Dr. Blem's wife, Leann, calls it.

Dr. Blem is wrapping up a 12-year study of the energetics of three species of water snake that cohabit in the southeastern corner of Virginia:

brown water snakes, Northern water snakes and cottonmouths. Such a study requires field work, which, in this case, involves floating around swamps in a canoe and plucking snakes out of trees.

I've been out with Dr. Blem for his annual spring snake hunt twice, and it's the kind of experience that makes being a scientist look like fun. This year we had a beautiful spring day and a high tide, enabling us to get way back up in various fingers of the creek. Dr. Blem is editor of an ornithological journal, so canoeing with him is an education in birds, too.

In four hours we saw a record 72 snakes. That's 18 snakes per hour! They were hanging in the bushes everywhere! Of those 72 snakes, 64 were brown water snakes, which, let me tell you, are a good copy of a cottonmouth.

Dr. Blem collected a few browns for his study, using his hands, a long pair of tongs or, once, a noose rigged on the end of a fishing pole. He doesn't mess around with the poisonous snakes, though. "C-mouths" get the tong treatment.

Around here, cottonmouths are the odd man out and getting odder. Although you can find cottonmouths in every creek in the deep South, in Virginia they occur only in pockets along the Appomattox River, around Virginia Beach and in the Newport News City Park. In more than 500 hours of field work, Dr. Blem has only about 300 cottonmouth sightings, compared to some 1,200 brown sightings.

Dr. Blem thinks there are few cottonmouths locally because snakes in Virginia must hibernate and cottonmouths don't do that very well. Still, the local population has held its own until recent years, when the snake's main predators --bulldozers and shotguns -- have put a lot of pressure on it.

One small colony near Hopewell disappeared when its hibernation grounds were bulldozed. On our recent outing, we didn't see the first cottonmouth. "The conditions were perfect and that was our best location, too," Dr. Blem said.

What we did see was a new road cut down to the previously inaccessible hibernation mounds.

"It's a fragile population. Developers build on their hibernation sites, then they come up in somebody's back yard and get clubbed," Blem said.

"And we have some hobbyists who think it's fun to shotgun snakes. They claim to have killed hundreds.

"Between the snake hunting and the destruction of habitat, if you come back in 10 years you'll have browns but I bet the cottonmouths will be virtually gone."

Because of the authority of Charlie Blem, I am able to assert with confidence that there are no cottonmouths in Goochland County. Because I am possessed of this one fact about a certain species of poisonous snake, I have acquired the reputation of An Authority on Snakes. People call me all the time to identify snakes over the telephone.

Jonna Barber called me up one night from her barn and described a small snake she had hacked to death with a hoe. "Do you think it's poisonous?" she asked.

"I don't know, but it doesn't matter now."

Last summer Sherry Sackett called and wanted me to come identify a snake skin she'd found in the rafters of her basement. I knew there was a big black rat snake that lived under her house and suggested the skin was his, but Sherry said, No, the skin was mottled.

That was intriguing, so I went over for a look. The skin was folded back and forth behind a joist, so I took a stick and gently pulled it out. It was freshly shed and held together as I pulled...and pulled and pulled. We laid it on the ground to measure and it was six full feet of black snake skin. The mottling Sherry saw was the dark eyes of the scales shining against the light interstices.

The first summer I lived in Goochland, I shared quarters with a number of varmints who didn't realize their cottage had a new resident. One of these was a small black snake that came in through a knot hole in the floor under the sofa. The first time I saw him he was coiled up on the rug and I nearly stepped on him.

It was a particularly inopportune time for a snake to appear in the living room, because I was expecting company momentarily. The company was a fellow from the Midwest who was making his first visit to Virginia. Naturally, I was eager to show him how we live in Virginia, and my image of how we live in Virginia did not include having snakes in the living room.

As I stood over this uninvited guest, trying to think of a tactful (and effective) way to ask him to leave, the snake sensed that he was persona non grata and he retired to the powder room. He struck a pose on the bath mat and I decided to wrap him up in the mat and throw the mat out the door.

I climbed onto the lavatory and over to the commode, from which I leaned down and took hold of the edge of the bath mat. The snake shot back into the living room.

For some lengthy period of time following, I chased the snake around the house. He kept trying to go for the sofa and his knot hole exit, but I thought he wanted to hide in the cushions only to reappear at an even more inopportune time, so I headed him off.

It was not a constant chase. It went in fits and starts. The snake would move and I would start. Fearful of knocking over lamps and bric-a-brac in my fright, I moved breakable items to the safety of the sofa. Pretty soon, everything in the living room was piled on top of the sofa and the snake and I were squared off in an open arena.

We circled each other several times, the snake spitting out his tongue and trying--very successfully--to unnerve me. Time was running out, so I laid a towel over my hands and prepared to grab the snake by the neck. It was one of the three most terrifying things I've ever done. My knees were, as in the best thrillers, knocking.

But I grabbed him and threw him, towel and all, out the door.

I retired, shaken, to a kitchen chair where the company from the Midwest found me babbling to myself.

He was fascinated to see how we live in Virginia--with all the lamps, tables and bric-a-brac piled on the living room sofa.

CHAPTER 11

Sometimes Ya Just Gotta Go

en days ago, Lake Andrews and I were sitting in two of the thousands of chairs arranged on the Mall in front of the United States Capitol. In front of us, barely within binocular range, was a white podium with the Presidential seal, flanked on both sides by galleries of Congressmen and -women.

We could make out on the podium the leader of the free world, his wife, his successor and several members of the Supreme Court, identifiable at that distance by the snap of their robes in the stiff wind.

Towering precariously over this august assemblage on each side was scaffolding for the media, many of whose representatives surely had nosebleeds.

Next to us sat the mayor of Elkhart, Ind., who was, of course, a constituent of former Senator, now Vice President Dan Quayle. The mayor was also a Democrat who had been an elector for Michael Dukakis, but he seemed to be having a good time, none the less.

On the other side of us was a couple from San Antonio who confirmed all of the stereotypical images of Texans. Sam, who had been one of President Bush's three finance chairmen in Texas, had on a cowboy hat and boots with his overcoat. Anne, who was chewing gum, had on a fur coat, sterling silver earrings and a pear-shaped diamond ring so large it put cubic zirconium to shame.

Behind us was a sea of humanity washing halfway back down the Mall. Above us, the air was filled with helicopters, grey clouds and patriotic music.

Sam and Anne had been in Washington all week attending the various gala functions. They had particularly enjoyed the entertainment at the Kennedy Center the night before. "It was so hokie, it was wonderful," Sam said.

Then, nodding toward the podium, he said, "The parties were fun, but this is what we came for."

You came all the way from Texas to sit out in a freezing wind for two hours and squint at figures a half mile away?

Sam and Anne could have watched the swearing-in on television from a comfortable hotel room. Lake and I could have watched it from a cozy den with a fire. Millions of people did watch on television, and they must have been happy to have avoided the crowded subways, long lines at the security check points and a wintry day.

Several people that I had asked to go with me said they preferred the electronic experience to being there in person.

"You can't see anything," they protested.

Yes, but...

But there is more to such events than seeing the pores on the President's face. There's a bigger picture than a 25-inch screen can capture.

Historical diaries and docudramas are full of instances of people walking 50 or 100 miles to see Abraham Lincoln and Stephen A. Douglas debate or to see the train car carrying President Garfield's body home to Ohio. These were the major events of the day, and people wanted to be part of them.

Vast improvements in transportation and communications have made it unnecessary for anyone to walk three days to see the President of the United States or any other luminary. Nowadays, people will hardly walk out the front door to see the President of the United States. Ironically, as it has become easier to attend historic events and see famous people, it has become less imperative to do so.

The Super Bowl and Michael Jackson concerts are about the only events that can stir us out of our armchairs.

People don't attend historic events in person because the experience is thought to be available on television. Yes, television brings the action closer, but it is an edited, controlled version. That is the danger, that this controlled experience will be taken for the real thing.

Television, for instance, can't deliver the private conversation of the Midwestern mayor or the Texas supporter who might be sitting near you. Television can't deliver the sense of being part of a big, diverse country that for one moment was united.

In its early days, television had tremendous impact. People watched Presidential speeches and felt they knew their leader better. People watched Jack Ruby shoot Lee Harvey Oswald and they were horrified. People watched Neil Armstrong walk on the Moon and they were awed.

But after 40 years, television has saturated our senses and, in the process, trivialized every heretofore exciting or historic event.

Hollywood agents used to worry about overexposure of their clients. They knew that which was rare held more interest for the public. Thanks to television, no event or public figure today suffers from underexposure. Every night on the six o'clock news, we see stories about a heinous murder, a state team winning the championship, the Governor appointing a woman to high office, the bankruptcy of a major corporation, a bombing by foreign terrorists and the launching of a spaceship.

Before the advent of television, these stories would have constituted a year's worth of excitement. A hundred years ago, they would have constituted the highlights of an entire lifetime.

Now we have so many such incidents covered so thoroughly by television that it takes a dedicated viewer to keep up with all the excitement. And over the years, we've become jaded by the once-in-a-lifetime events that happen three times a day in living color in our living room.

Television is not really the villain. Television has simply fulfilled its promise too well.

Ronald Reagan is as familiar to us as our next door neighbor. We know his voice, his expressions, his mannerisms so well, what could drive us to leave the television close-up in order to hear his voice over a microphone and catch a blurry glimpse of his face through binoculars?

And yet, by being there, we become part of the event. The people who spent January 20, 1989 in front of the Capitol weren't passive spectators; they were participants in an historic moment. It's sort of like having guests at a wedding. The witnesses, by their sheer numbers, give weight to the proceedings. By "helping" George Bush be sworn in as President, they reminded each other and the elected officials on the dais that this is a government of, by and for the people.

In retrospect, the only thing Lake and I missed by being at the inauguration in person was hearing a commentator explain that the parade was starting late because a doughnut concessionaire's truck was on fire.

On the other hand, had I settled for the electronic experience, I would have missed:

* The spontaneity of tens of thousands of citizens leaping to their feet at the conclusion of the oath of office, whooping and cheering for President George Bush.

* The poignancy of tens of thousands of departing spectators stopping to wave silently at the helicopter carrying former President Ronald Reagan away from Washington.

* And of course, the considerable surprise of finding myself walking away from the Capitol shoulder to shoulder with Donald Trump.

Some things can't be transmitted over airwaves. Sometimes ya just gotta be there.

CHAPTER 12

An Open Letter to Queen Elizabeth

Dear Queen,

I know you're busy planning the rehearsal dinner before the wedding of your son, young Charlie Windsor, and that cute little trick he's engaged to, Lady Diana Spencer, so I won't take much of your time. I've been reading about their courtship and looking at the pictures of them in the paper, and they make a mighty handsome couple. I did read something that worried me, though, and I decided to pass along my thoughts, for what they're worth. My daddy always told me free advice was worth what you paid for it, so maybe I ought to send you a bill with this, ha ha.

Our paper ran a little piece the other day saying that Lady Diana thought polo was "boring" and she wanted Charlie to quit playing. I knew as soon as I read it that horses wasn't the problem. Didn't I read somewhere that she cried when Charlie's favorite horse died? No sirree bobtail, it's not horses so much as jealousy. Diana doesn't want Charlie spending so much time sporting around on the polo field where maybe he'll fall in with a bad crowd. She wants him to herself. (Isn't that just like a woman?--fall in love with a fellow because he's exciting and devilish and then, as soon as he's hooked, set about changing the things that caught her fancy to begin with.)

You being a horsewoman, I figured you'd realize the seriousness of the situation and step in before things got out of hand. But right away there was another story about Charlie talking it over with one of his friends, saying he didn't know what to do because his lady friend "really hates it."

Now Queen, you or your boy, one, has got to have a talk with that girl or you might as well call the whole thing off now. Believe me, I know what I'm talking about. My oldest girl married a boy from Arkansas who liked to coon hunt at night on mules. He didn't do it much while they were courting because he was over here to see her every night, but after they got married, he started hunting two or three nights a week. Of course, then he had to take extra time to look after his mule, and he bought a couple of coon dogs of his own --and let me tell you, coon dogs aren't cheap. I think he spent $400 apiece on them -- and he spent a lot of time hanging around with these other characters who hunted with him. It was a right rough bunch, drank too much. Well, the next thing you know, he wanted to carry that mule and those $400 dogs over to Louisiana for some big hunt they were having down there and my daughter just put her foot down. "It's that mule or me," she told him.

Don't you know that boy took his mule and left her? And they had a big church wedding, too, like I'm sure Charlie and Diana are going to have.

Now I don't know what I'm going to do. My wife is all to pieces about having a divorce in the family, and I don't know where I'm going to find another husband for my oldest girl. The other two are pretty enough to make out on their own.

Anyway, I'm sure you can see what I'm driving at. Those horse people put their horse first and their wife second.

The way I see it, you've got a no-win situation. If Diana asks Charlie to choose between her and polo and he takes her, then you've got a wimp for the next king. If he takes the horses, then you've got a divorce on your hands. I know that's easier than beheading her, ha ha, but not much. It's expensive, too. (I know a fellow here who'll handle everything for $150 if it's not contested, and I'll be glad to put you in touch with him if it comes to that).

Think how messy a divorce would be, though. Charlie would have to hang around outside the royal enclosure at Ascot when you all went to the races and that would look pretty shabby. Dividing up all the presents is tough, too. You just can't split the blanket, ha ha.

And what if they had children? Thank goodness my girl was taking those pills and she didn't have any. Maybe you should tell Diana to take them for a couple of years until they see if it works out. If she won't, then you run the risk of having juvenile delinquents for grandchildren. Think how embarrassing it would be to have your own grandchild hauled into court for smoking that pot, all because his momma didn't like horses.

I'm telling you, this horse thing is serious business. (I know another couple this happened to, only it was the wife who rode. Now she's happily married to a real nice fellow who likes horses, too.) You and Mr. Windsor talk it over and see what you think. I just don't want to see you two having to go through what we're going through. Maybe Lady Diana would be just as happy to marry one of your other boys (if he doesn't ride). I'm sure Charlie can find somebody else. My youngest girl likes horses and she wouldn't mind moving to England.

Yours truly, Hezekiah Danzler

P.S. My wife said your husband's name is Mr. Mountbatten and I said I never figured the queen of England for one of those liberated types who keeps her own name, ha ha.

CHAPTER 13

Victim of Lucy Andrews Syndrome
Sees 'Snowy Hawk'

There is a condition known as Lucy Andrews Syndrome that runs in our family. This perverse condition manifests itself by afflicting the people around the person who has it. It is characterized by an uncontrollable urge to fill in the blanks and to answer even rhetorical questions. Victims of Lucy Andrews Syndrome are often called, erroneously, know-it-alls.

The eponymous victim of Lucy Andrews Syndrome was a little old lady in Orange County who raised horses and Cain. Lucy Andrews was a Colorful Character who took great delight in supplying answers to questions. In Lucy, this behavior was more of a fine art than an affliction.

It was her firm belief that when people asked a question, they wanted an answer, right, wrong or even unreasonable. She would often give outrageous replies or interpretations of situations, just to provide an answer to a question. The thing was, sometimes she was right, so you couldn't dismiss her statements out of hand.

One time she and I drove to a Thoroughbred sale in Timonium, Md. As we drove under the lattice of overpasses around Washington and Baltimore, I noticed the streets above us seemed to be named for people. Making idle conversation, I said, "I wonder who Charles M. Conrad was?"

Lucy replied thoughtfully, "I believe he was Secretary of War under Millard Fillmore."

I couldn't believe Lucy Andrews, of all people, would know who Millard Fillmore's cabinet members were. On the other hand, I didn't either, so I couldn't call her on it. This is the epitome of LAS, a statement that couldn't possibly be true, but that no one has the facts to refute.

Victims of LAS aren't practical jokers -- that would imply premeditation. These statements just pop out of their mouths. It's all in the delivery. What happens is people with LAS say things with such assurance that, in the absence of evidence to the contrary, their opinions are taken as fact.

Lucy Andrews Syndrome is fairly widespread, attacking nearly half of all Americans. Studies of married couples have shown that, in almost every case, one partner has Lucy Andrews Syndrome.

In our marriage, I'm the one with LAS, but my husband is the one who suffers from it.

This is the way it happens:

One night we were awakened by a pained, mournful cry emanating from the front pasture. Neither one of us had ever heard this cry before, and naturally we were curious about its source.

We looked out the window and in the moonlight we could see the horses approaching the spot where the cry came from. "It's a dying buzzard," I said with authority and put on my clothes to go see.

Cricket wisely offered no opinion but followed me into the pasture with the flashlight. There we picked up the shiny green eyes of...not a dying buzzard...but a fox! She trotted casually away from us, stopping once or twice to look back. It turned out to be a vixen teaching her cubs to hunt, and we heard her calling them and coaching them frequently over the summer.

Of course, that wasn't anything like a dying buzzard, as Cricket cheerfully pointed out. After so many years, Cricket has learned to recognize my attacks of LAS. He will hold his tongue early on but when I am proven wrong, he'll crow over it.

One night recently we were up at the Pole with Jerri and Bob Marx. In the course of the conversation, Bob used the word "erudite." That was fine until I said "erudition."

"Isn't that a verb?" Cricket questioned, and my tongue muscles started tingling the way they do during an outbreak of Lucy Andrews Syndrome.

"No," I said semi-facetiously, "the verb is eruditize."

One of the things about LAS is that a statement like that pretty much stops the conversation. The recipients of this specious "fact" pause to consider its validity, all the while studying the face of the LAS person for tell-tale signs of twitching tongue muscles. Such is the authoritative tone-of-voice of LAS victims that their statements usually stand, doubted maybe, but not controverted.

Rossie Fisher reports that her husband, Sandy, had an attack of Lucy Andrews Syndrome during their vacation at Sanibel Island. They saw a beautiful large brown-and-white bird and Rossie said, "What kind of bird do you suppose that is?"

Eager to satisfy his wife's curiosity by providing an answer, any answer, Sandy said authoritatively, "It's a snowy hawk."

Rossie said she just gave him a long does-he-know-something-I-don't-know look.

My mother has a variation of LAS that has to do with filling out forms. This is a beneficial form of the condition that helps people deal with red tape without losing their minds.

If getting something done means filling out a form, Momma is the person to call. She will fill out any form and answer every question, completely unfettered by facts. She has an instinctive understanding of bureaucrats and computers. Neither bureaucrats nor computers care whether the data they receive is any good, as long as all the blanks are filled in.

When I was growing up, social security numbers were just coming into general use. Momma didn't have one and she didn't know what Daddy's number was, so any time a form asked for her social security number, she made one up.

When I went to work and got a number, I left the card with my number in the silver chest. For years after that, Momma would get out my card and copy my social security number whenever she needed one.

My daddy used to be on the road all week, and Momma found running the household in his absence often required something more than filling out forms. Sometimes it required forging Daddy's signature.

My fifteenth birthday, that magical day when I became legally old enough to have a driver's license, fell on a Monday. After school, Momma drove me to the Division of Motor Vehicles office for this rite of passage. I filled out the form, she signed it and we gave it to the clerk.

The clerk said, "You have to have both parents' signatures." (This was obviously in the days before divorce had been invented.)

Well, Daddy was in Madison, Wisconsin, or somewhere for the week, and I was consumed with the disappointment that only a teenager can feel at the prospect of having to wait four whole days to get her driver's license.

Momma didn't change her expression. She took the form back from the clerk and said, "Okay."

Then we went out and drove around the block, where she stopped long enough to sign Daddy's name on the form. I was amazed at her audacity, thrilled at her ability to get around the red tape and certain we would be hung up by our thumbs if we were caught, which we probably would be. When I gasped something to that effect, she shrugged. "They don't know but what your Daddy's office is two blocks from the DMV."

Coolness in the face of possible exposure is a sign of Lucy Andrews Syndrome.

Momma's defense has always been that she's trying to expedite matters. It works. She's gotten more done than anybody I know, and I've tried to emulate her methods, filling out forms creatively as necessary.

I've seldom been called on to forge my husband's signature, which is lucky because there's no way I could even approximate it. However, I can forge my daddy's signature perfectly, should the need ever arise.

CHAPTER 14

Great Expectations:
The Truth about Pregnancy

o start with, there's more to being pregnant than getting fat and smiling beatifically. You have to put up with a myriad of, shall we say, physical inconveniences. And then there's all the advice from friends and other people that you have to listen to, not mention the war stories.

There's a reason women wait awhile to reveal that they are expecting a baby. When you reveal that you are pregnant, you instantly become part of the Sisterhood, the initiation rites of which consist of being forced to hear endless recitals of labor, childbirth and other bodily functions. It is absolutely astonishing the intimate things near strangers will tell you.

In the seven months since I was officially declared pregnant, I'll bet I've heard how every child within 100 miles of Richmond came into the world. One woman even told me about conception: "It was during Hurricane Zelma and our apartment building was surrounded by water and we couldn't get out, so my husband and I just did it."

"Your husband delivered your baby?"

"No," she said, "we made the baby."

All of which seems very unreal during the first three or four months of pregnancy. It's hard to imagine that because you are throwing up and napping three times a day you are going to have a permanent houseguest six months hence.

It was particularly hard for me because I've never been interested in babies, per se. I've always had a strong feeling about having children of my own, but in an abstract sort of way. By that I mean I've never pictured myself cuddling an infant, nor have I had fatuous fantasies about being a mother.

On the rare occasions when I pictured myself with offspring, I envisioned a seven-year-old on a pony. I love kittens and puppies and foals but babies don't do anything for me. All I know is that you don't have to wait 10 days for them to open their eyes.

Nevertheless, I was eager enough to have children with my husband that I had surgery and spent six years enduring numerous treatments and tests to get to this point. The long wait and the repeated discouragement probably accounted for my doubts about whether I was really having a baby or not. It seemed like a hoax and for a long time I half expected the doctor to call and tell me the pregnancy test was wrong.

One day I looked down and saw that I was wearing a jumper and knee socks and decided I really was pregnant. That is the uniform, isn't it?

Keeping yourself clothed is one of the major problems of pregnancy.

The first thing I did was swear off pantyhose. The over-the-knee, elastic top stockings I bought at the dime store were vastly more comfortable, but they required some concessions to vanity. One day when I had done a lot of walking around at lunch time, my stockings fell down in puddles around my ankles just as I got on the elevator.

Momma had bought the jumper for me early on and I laughed because I figured I'd never be big enough to fill it up. I thought I could be 17 months pregnant and still wear it. You could make a three-man tent out of it in a pinch. It was so long, you didn't even need knee-highs, you could wear hightop shoes.

The first few times I riffled through maternity racks were depressing, to say the least. The designers of maternity clothes have been reading too many articles about the high percentage of teenaged mothers-to-be. Everything I saw either had teddy bears and choo-choo trains on the front or designs that I can only assume were taken from punk rock performers. There was nothing for a 37-year-old with tailored taste.

One disastrous afternoon I went looking for a shorty nightie. I finally found one I liked, but it came in only two sizes: my normal size and hippopotamus. I figured I'd outgrow my normal size in another week, so I tried on the hippopotamus size and almost cried. The panties came down to my knees. They looked sort of like nylon boxer shorts for a Sumo wrestler. In a fit of misplaced practicality, I bought the set.

Naturally, it fits perfectly these days.

I was also in the market for larger bras. But I found out when you go from a respectable 34 to a 36 or 38, you are moving into the realm of massive structural restraints. As I gazed at the racks of...of equipment, I kept thinking of a civil engineering course my brother took in college called "Stresses and Strains." At the juncture of 34s and 36s on the display racks, a lascivious sea of lacy, colored lingerie crashes abruptly into a shimmering white bulkhead of serious bras.

The manufacturers of size 36 and larger bras take a serious approach to their responsibility to provide structural stability. Size 36 bras have three-inch wide straps and a bank of hooks in back that would put a corset to shame. The band under the cups extends down to your navel. Lace has been rejected as too flimsy for the task of molding mounds of mammary into upswept pyramids. Serious bras are made of some industrial-strength material similar to that found in two-ply, steel-belted radials. The manufacturers have even eschewed dye, I suppose because it weakens the fabric.

I skipped the bras and went home to order a set of "bra extenders" from Miles Kimball.

Shoes eventually became a problem, too. One day my ankles disappeared. I had always heard your feet and ankles swelled during pregnancy, but I doubted it would happen to me. (I was mistaken about several other aspects of this condition, too.) Anyway, my toes look like little sausages and I can't wear any of my shoes. So I went to the bargain shoe store and bought some white pumps and some iridescent pink tennies two whole sizes bigger to tide me over.

Because I'm such an old prima gravida, the doctors have tested me to death. I've had four ultrasounds and amniocentesis and alpha-fetal-protein check, among other things. I have a Polaroid-type picture of the fetus from the first ultrasound, but all you can see is a gray blob --kind of like the Rorschach inkblot test.

Still, it is the first baby picture.

The latest ultrasound was done at around five months. My husband went with me to see the baby. We were taken into the ultrasound room by a lively technician whose first words, as she set up the equipment, were:

"Would you like a video tape for five dollars?" I felt like we were at Kings Dominion, but we laughed and said yes.

It is amazing to look at the monitor and see the baby inside your stomach. We had a clear picture of her sucking her thumb and kicking her legs. I could feel her moving as I saw it on the screen, and that made me laugh, which made the picture bounce up and down.

We showed the tape to all our friends for a couple of weeks. Now it's being distributed through Video World.

Seeing the baby and feeling her move help me believe that yes, this really is happening. Even at eight months, I still look in the mirror in amazement. After all those years of disappointment...

I first felt the baby move at about four months. I was resting and felt several twinges below my navel near the surface. I did an inventory of my organs and concluded it had to be the baby. I wasn't sure I would recognize the feeling, as my pregnancy book gave numerous descriptions (butterflies, upset stomach, etc.). I mentioned that to Momma, and she said in her inimitably down-to-earth way, "It feels like someone inside you kicking around."

Well, of course.

I've gotten used to feeling the baby move around now, but at first it was kind of creepy to think there was a little person inside my stomach. It was like having worms or something weird out of a sci-fi movie.

Now, with a month to go, the movements are a reassuring sign that my baby is growing and getting fit. I can feel her running all over my insides. Someone gave her the Jane Fonda Pregnancy Workout tape and she does that about 15 times a day.

It's a hoot to lie back and watch your stomach bouncing around. It looks like kittens playing under the covers. Of course, sometimes she does her calisthenics while I'm sitting around in public. I wish she wouldn't do that. It seems so unladylike.

One of my friends likes to feel the baby move. She sits by me and I put her hands on my stomach where I feel the most activity and we wait. There she sits with an other-worldly look of concentration on her face and her hands resting gently on my stomach like it was a Ouija Board.

My friends say they enjoy seeing me fat for a change, but I don't feel fat. If this protrusion were fat, it would fold over or squeeze out the sides when I bend over. This is more like having a volleyball tied to your middle: a fairly firm lump that doesn't fold or bend. It means you have to do things like weeding the garden on your hands and knees.

Fatigue has been my biggest complaint about pregnancy. I went through a phase of taking three naps a day. I felt like a 78 record being played at 33 1/3. They say being pregnant in the summer is the pits and it's true. Six weeks of relentless heat and humidity this summer really dragged me down. It was frustrating because I kept thinking I would become acclimated. I tended to look on pregnancy as an extended disability, an illness I was slow recovering from. Boy, was I slow!

As tired as I've been most of the time, I dread going to bed at night. Sleeping is such a project when you're pregnant. In the fourth and fifth months, I had insomnia. I dared not nap during the day, although I was stumbling around semi-comatose, because I'd be up all night.

I usually got up at 2 a.m. and roamed around the house feeding cats and putting dogs outside. Then I'd read awhile. Finally I found a long and hideously boring book -- "The Great Getty" by Robert Lenzner -- that got me through that period. Every time Lenzner began explaining Getty's stock transfers and financial manipulations, I dozed right off.

Here at the end, getting comfortable in bed is a lot of work. Pregnant women are not known for their agility, and this is compounded by lying down. Rolling over is a feat in itself. You have to kind of thrash around until you get your middle-heavy body flopped over on the desired side. Then you have to raise up and straighten out your nightgown, which is all wadded up under you. Then you have to arrange the extra pillows under your knees and your stomach. Finally, you lie there panting and your husband says in alarm, "Are you all right?"

Then, just as you doze off, the baby kicks you four or five times and says, Ma! Roll over! You're squushing me!

So you roll over and fix your nightgown and fix your pillows and pant and tell your husband you're okay and doze off. And then you have to get up and go to the bathroom.

Whenever I get to sleep for a few hours in a row, I have bizarre dreams. My family will tell you I've always been a great dreamer, but being pregnant has taken me to new heights of dreaming. One night I dreamed I had three goose eggs which hatched out 10 little chickens. I was upset, naturally, because we had already told people we were having a little girl.

If I don't have this baby soon, we're not going to have any china or glasses left. Either that or I'm going to burn the house down. The circulation in my hands is so poor because of fluid retention that I don't have much feeling in my fingers. So I break a glass or plate every day.

I also burn a lot of meals, not because of my hands but because I'm so absent-minded. I'll put a pan of diced potatoes on to boil -- on high, of course -- and leave. Go for a walk. Go to the barn. When I return, the water's gone, the pan's black inside and out, and I have to scrape the unburnt tops off the potatoes for supper.

Smoked mashed potatoes. My husband was a Boy Scout. I'll bet he's had them before.

When you're expecting a baby, people want you to do just that --expect the baby -- preferably in a white heat of excitement for the whole nine months. As soon as you find out you're pregnant, practice saying how excited you are. DO NOT consider telling anybody anything about your ambivalence. Never mind that every other mother-to-be has felt the same thing. You will get strange looks, or worse.

People want you to get ready for the baby, too. They want you to pick out names, furnish and decorate a nursery, buy a layette (whatever that is), take classes in parenting and childbirth, and enroll the child in private school. If anyone asks you about any of those preparations, just say it's all taken care of. DO NOT be drawn into divulging details.

For instance, NEVER tell ANYONE the baby's name before he's born. You are just asking for trouble. There are two kinds of people in the world: those who think parents ought to use family names exclusively, regardless of the burden this places on the child, and those who think parents ought to pick euphonic names out of the air, regardless of the burden this places on the child. No matter which side you're on, everyone you talk to will be on the other side.

And about those childbirth classes. We didn't take any, which is nothing short of heresy these days. I for one didn't want to hear another word about childbirth. And I couldn't see subjecting my husband to movies of strange women spewing out babies. After all, he's already said his contribution to childbirth will be to pace up and down the hall and smoke lots of cigarettes.

Unfortunately, we've told people our mutual decision to have this baby the old-fashioned, dignified way, where the husband waits outside until it's over. What a storm of controversy that has brought on!

I can't quite get tuned in to this idea that childbirth is a mystic experience, although it's possible I'll understand once I've been through it. I've delivered horses and dogs and I've seen a woman delivered at home by a midwife, and none of the mothers involved seemed to be having a mystic experience to me.

My attitude is that this is the way the baby gets from the inside to the outside and I would like for that process to be as safe for me and the baby as possible and, insofar as is compatible with safety, as painless as possible. To that end, I told my doctor that I wanted him to direct the show and that I wasn't going to tell him how to do his job.

Needless to say, I'm his favorite patient.

My mother's biggest concern in all this is that I be sufficiently drugged. She was dismayed to learn that they don't knock you out with ether anymore. She was doubtful about this spinal block/epidural business until a friend of mine delivered recently with it. Momma called me excitedly and said, "Edie had an epidural and said it was wonderful!"

Later I learned Edie had a baby, too.

When I told my brother I was keeping a journal about this experience, he said, "Well, I know it'll be funny, because you're not the gushy type."

This might sound gushy, but I have found there is one indispensable item for dealing with pregnancy: my husband's support. I cannot imagine why anyone would want to do this without a husband. I'm just talking about being pregnant. I haven't even gotten to the baby part yet.

My pregnancy has, as pregnancies go, been easy and uncomplicated. But compared to normal life, it's been something of an ordeal. My husband's help with chores, his consideration of how I feel at any time, and most of all, his excitement over the baby have been the saving grace of the past seven months. Sharing his happiness has made it all worthwhile.

Shared happiness is what started all this, as I recall.

Now, if I can just figure out what a layette is...

CHAPTER 15

Alexandra Ripley,
I Don't Give a Damn

So we're going to have a sequel to "Gone with the Wind," which Harry Ware says is like writing a sequel to the Bible. For a bid of $4.9 million, Warner Books has bought the right to publish the continuing saga of Rhett and Scarlett as written by Alexandra Ripley ("Charleston").

In the great scheme of things, I suppose this is nothing to fret about, but it really does distress me. I'm one of those people, obviously few in number, who believe the only person who could write a sequel to GWTW is Margaret Mitchell, who, unfortunately, was run over by a taxi in 1939, and is unavailable for the task.

Mitchell herself did not want a sequel, her estate does not want a sequel and nobody who has read and appreciated the book wants a sequel, either. Nevertheless, to avoid a rash of unauthorized sequels when the copyright runs out in 2011, Mitchell's brother reluctantly approved the Ripley rip-off.

The irony of all this is that they are going to do a sequel to the book. Ripley, for enough money and potential renown, is willing to commit the lese majesty of "finishing" Margaret Mitchell's chef d'oeuvre.

Why, oh why don't they just do a sequel to the movie? The people who care about books wouldn't mind and the people who don't care about books (the vast majority of people in the world) wouldn't know the difference.

The public will expect a continuation of the lives of the characters in the movie, not those in the book, who, let me assure you, are much more complex and interesting. If Alexandra Ripley somehow manages to write about the real Scarlett, all those thousands of readers who have never read the original are going to be in for a shock.

Making a movie out of a book, they say, is like making an armchair out of a sofa. It just ain't the same piece of furniture.

Some movie adaptations are pretty good -- GWTW is at least faithful to the basic plot -- and some bear little resemblance to the original product.

Books and movies are distinct media. For one thing, scriptwriters nearly always seem to feel movies should have a "popular" ending. A book which ends with the death of the hero or the parting of the lovers will, when transformed into a movie, not.

Burt Reynolds made a psychological Western called "The Man Who Loved Cat Dancing," at the end of which, after being hunted down by men determined not to bring him back alive, he is left wounded in a cave to be tended by his lover, with whom he will presumably live happily ever after. In the book, he dies.

But since nobody reads the book anymore, scriptwriters get away with that sort of nonsense.

Another problem in the transmogrification of a book into a movie is that there are things you can do in writing that you can't do on film, and vice versa. A prime example of that is "Heartburn." Nora Ephron wrote this thinly disguised story of her marriage to and divorce from Carl Bernstein (as in "Woodward and..."), and two of my favorite performers, Meryl Streep and Jack Nicholson, made the movie version.

The novel was written in first person, which is automatically impossible to do on the screen, unless you have the main character walking around talking to himself all the time, which isn't very satisfactory. Despite Ephron's sad story, the book was funny because of the way it was written. Unable to convey the humorous first person point of view, the movie was depressing.

I really do love Jack Nicholson, but he obviously never reads the book, because he played in another bastardization, "Terms of Endearment." This is a rare example of the movie's being superior to the book. I'm a big fan of Larry McMurty's work -- "Lonesome Dove" is certainly worthy of the Pulitzer it won -- but he lost me with "Terms of Endearment."

Nevertheless, I gave the movie a try. The movie was better because, for one thing, the chronology was handled more smoothly. But -- get this -- the character played by Nicholson is a total fabrication. He doesn't appear in the book at all, not by name, not by profession, not by personality. I spent the whole 129 minutes wondering where he came from and whether this was the right videotape.

By now, you have probably guessed correctly that I love books and I am often distressed by their treatment as movies. I have found over the years that it's best to see the movie first and then indulge myself with the book. Otherwise, I find myself disturbing other theater patrons with remarks like, "No, no, Frank didn't return to London when he'd made his fortune; he bought a farm in Australia. And why doesn't Lewis have a twin sister?"

The all-time biggest offenders in the book-to-movie travesty contest are the producers of the "Tarzan" movies. I read, loved and memorized all 22 volumes in Edgar Rice Burroughs' series on Tarzan of the apes. The first two books were far and away the best, but the sequels were fun, too.

The Johnnie Weissmuller-vintage movies were acutely embarrassing to me. As a child I was genuinely distressed at what I saw as the comic portrayal of my hero. Here was the Lord of the Jungle dressed in rags and spouting inanities like, "Me Tarzan, you Jane," when in the reality of the book he spoke perfect French. He was also literate in English, and he later learned to speak German. The upsetting thing was that the celluloid Tarzan behaved in the Neanderthal way his diction suggested.

Ah, but the record was set straight finally with "Greystoke," was it not?

It was not. The producers got the part about Tarzan's youth and transition to civilization right, but they forgot that this was essentially an adventure story, and they left Lord Greystoke to rot in Scotland, not the site of Tarzan's better-known adventures.

So who knows what drivel Alexandra Ripley will feed an idiotic public in "Son of Tara" or "Dynasty Goes to Georgia," or whatever Warner Books decides to call the sequel to GWTW.

And of course tens of thousands of people who have never read the original will read the sequel, drawn to it by visions of Clark Gable carrying Vivian Leigh up the Jefferson Hotel staircase. The public will expect a continuation of the lives of the characters in the movie, not those in the book. And I'm fearful that Alexandra Ripley will give them exactly that.

Although I've enjoyed the movie over the years, recently I've begun to feel the same embarrassment for Scarlett that I felt for Tarzan. The movie makes Scarlett out to be a saucy minx who manipulates men for her selfish ends, not the resourceful woman who prospers in the face of incredible odds in the book.

And the movie leaves a somewhat melodramatic impression on people, based on the enduring popularity of two lines: Butterfly McQueen's "But Miss Scarlett, I don't know nothing 'bout birthin' babies" and Clark Gable's "Frankly, my dear, I don't give a damn."

But in the book, two of the most gripping lines are Scarlett's vow, "If I live through this, so help me God I'll never be hungry again," and her daddy's admonition to hold onto the land, "Nothing else matters."

It is unfashionable to find any redeeming qualities in any white person, real or literary, who lived in the South in the 19th century, but I confess to a great admiration for Katie Scarlett O'Hara.

I read the book five times in my teens and twenties and each time I grew to admire Scarlett more. Here was a woman who was raised in a very sheltered world, with little education, who suddenly found herself as the head of a houseful of people who would have starved to death without her leadership. In the wreckage of the war and "reconstruction," she survived and prospered because she recognized how the world had changed. She adapted, using the resources she had at hand, which happened to be feminine wiles and an innate business sense.

I've always found a wry amusement in the scorn that feminists have for the flirtatious Scarlett of the movie, because the Scarlett of the book is a wonderful example of an independent, self-determining woman. Like many such women in the current times, she found out too late that she had sacrificed her personal life for professional success.

In the end, I guess it doesn't matter what they do with Scarlett because the real Scarlett will always be there in the book for anyone to find.

CHAPTER 16

An Eye for an Eye,
An Eye for a Horse

Country people notice things. I don't know why that is, but it's true. It seems to me that city people have just as many things to be observant about as country people, but they just don't pay attention to what's around them.

My daddy says the most observant person he ever knew was Tom McKelvey. Tom McKelvey was a horse trader in Pennsylvania from whom my daddy bought a succession of horses in the '60s. Well, he didn't actually buy them outright. He bought them "on trial." He went off to Tom McKelvey's with an empty horse trailer one time and for 10 years thereafter he shuttled horses back and forth between Oxford, Pennsylvania and Lynchburg, Virginia.

Daddy bought his hunting horses there. Periodically he would bring home some Thoroughbred that couldn't run or had broken down at the track and that Tom McKelvey had patched up and spent, oh, most of one afternoon teaching to jump. Daddy would bring the horse home "on trial," hunt him for a couple of months and take him back to Tom McKelvey, who would generously take the horse back as a down payment on another graduate of his racehorse recycling program.

Tom McKelvey mass-produced hunting horses (and show hunters, too, no doubt) by teaching them to jump telephone poles in a corral. He stood in the middle cracking a whip and driving the horses around a chute on the rim of the corral. Spaced around the chute were good-sized, solid jumps made of telephone poles.

Daddy never offered an opinion of this training method, other than to say, "The casualty rate was high, but the ones that survived could jump a big fence."

In 1962, Tom McKelvey sold Daddy a series of bay Thoroughbred geldings, all of which are a blur in my memory. None of them stayed long enough to acquire a name. They ran in with the rest of our little herd and were referred to, respectively, as "New Horse," "New New Horse" and "New New New Horse."

I'm not sure there was anything wrong with them. Daddy just liked trading horses. When the mood struck him to trade, he could always come up with a good reason for trading.

He went through a spell of bing-bonging back and forth between Thoroughbreds and cold-blooded horses. He has a good eye for a horse and his weakness is a tall, flashy Thoroughbred. Whenever Tom McKelvey had such a horse, Daddy would bring him home "on trial."

Daddy would hunt the horse for a few weeks, and the horse would be hyper and pull and jerk and dance around until Daddy got disgusted and took him back to Tom McKelvey. He'd say, "This horse is so hot he takes all the pleasure out of hunting. Find me something cold-blooded that will stand quietly and let me enjoy myself."

So Tom McKelvey would send Daddy home with a half-Percheron and for a few weeks Daddy would enjoy hunting. He'd look at the horse's big haunches and laugh affectionately. "He's lonesome," Daddy would say, "lonesome for the plow."

Then he'd go off hunting with another club and suddenly he'd be embarrassed, as Master of Fox Hounds, to be riding a big old half-bred horse. Back he'd go to Oxford, Pa., and tell Tom McKelvey, "I can't be visiting these other hunts on a plow horse. Find me a tall, good-looking Thoroughbred."

And Tom McKelvey would...for a price.

"I never beat him on a single deal," Daddy says mournfully.

"Every horse I traded him required a thousand dollars' difference. Didn't matter if I was trading him a better horse than I was getting, which I was sometimes. It was always a thousand dollars to boot.

"I'd go up there knowing this time I was going to beat him. But I never did."

The closest he ever came to beating Tom McKelvey on a deal was the time he traded a big black mare named Patsy. Patsy was one of the "lonesome" ones, but she was good-looking and honest and could jump the biggest fence in Virginia. Patsy had been open jumper champion of eastern Pennsylvania but she wasn't quite sound when Tom McKelvey got her. He patched her up in his inimitable way and sold her to Daddy "on trial."

Well, the trial lasted several years, Patsy was that good. But eventually, the urge to trade overcame Daddy's affection for the mare and he called Tom McKelvey. Tom McKelvey said he could always find a home for a horse like Patsy and to bring her on back.

At that point in her life, Patsy had a few years and a few thousand jumps on her legs, and she was getting kind of creaky. But Daddy figured he could patch her up as well as Tom McKelvey could.

"When I took Patsy up there, I stopped outside of town and gave her a pill and took her out of the trailer and let her walk around so she wouldn't be stiff with her arthritis," Daddy recalled.

"When I got there, Tom said, 'I'm glad to get this old mare back. I've got just the man who wants her, if she's sound. Is she doing all right?' I said yeah, she's fine. So Tom said, 'Pull her out and let's have a look at her.'"

Anticipating his first victory in horsetrading with Tom McKelvey, Daddy said, "I unloaded her and she came out on three legs. She just hobbled around in front of his barn. I was so mad...and embarrassed. I said, 'She must have capped her hock in the trailer.' But I didn't fool him."

Tom McKelvey had herds of horses cycling through his place all the time, bays and chestnuts and grays, green horses, old horses, not-quite-sound horses. What always impressed Daddy about Tom McKelvey, in addition to his sharp trading, was that he remembered and recognized every horse that had ever been on his place.

"He had an eye like I never heard tell of," Daddy says every time Tom McKelvey's name comes up. Over all the years that Daddy went there, he saw many instances of Tom McKelvey's powers of observation. The one that made the man a legend, though, involved a cow, not a horse.

Tom McKelvey and Daddy had gone to visit a nearby dairy farm together, and as they were walking through a stanchion barn, past two long rows of cow rumps, Tom McKelvey stopped suddenly in back of a cow. Looking her over quickly, he turned to the dairyman and said, "You know, if that cow had horns, I'd swear it was the same cow I traded you that time."

And the dairyman said, "By God, that is the same cow. I had her dehorned."

Tom McKelvey's dead now, been dead for 10 or 15 years, but one of his horses is still around. The last horse Daddy got from him, the one he traded crippled Patsy for, is happily retired down the road from me. Ironsides, gray-gone-white, has been 25 years old since I moved to Goochland in 1976. He's one of the "lonesome" ones...and he can probably still jump a big fence.

CHAPTER 17

Grown-ups Don't Eat Cookie Dough

My mother kept my year-old daughter for a couple of days recently and when she handed the baby back to me, she said, "Now I've taught this child a new word and I don't want you to mess it up."

I was a little take aback by her serious tone and I said, "What did you teach her?"

Momma looked me in the eye and said, "I taught her 'no.' I'm sure she's never heard that word before in her life."

I laughed. "What heinous crime did she commit to bring this on?" I asked.

"She spit out her food."

I admitted to Momma that Katherine Bolling did that all the time and I didn't know how to make her stop. I did know enough not to laugh at her, although I wanted to. But I was truly amazed at the idea that telling her "no" would make her stop.

So that night when Katherine Bolling began blowing her pureed potatoes and chicken all over me, I sat up and barked in my best bad-dog voice, "No! No! Bad girl!"

Katherine Bolling looked at me in total astonishment for three seconds before spraying me again.

This incident has underscored for me the futility of my pretending to be an authority figure. I know I'm going to be one of those mothers who, as her child runs amok in her friend's living room, wrings her hands and says, "I can't do a thing with her."

I feel absolutely ridiculous being stern and telling children what to do. Being stern and telling children what to do is something grown-ups do, and I'm having a hard time believing I'm a grown-up.

Being 38 years old is not enough to make you feel grown up. Being 38 years old and married isn't enough, either. Being 38 years old, married, a homeowner, secretary of a garden club, a branch manager, a Sunday school teacher and a T-ball coach isn't enough, either, but it's getting close.

I've asked several people how to tell when you're grown up. My cousin Michael says you can tell you're grown up when you make your own dental appointments --and keep them.

Rebecca Gurlen says doing the flowers for church is the definitive criterion of grown-upness.

The electrician working on our house, Greg Casarotti, says wanting to play baseball and football and not being able to anymore makes him feel grown up. He also says sending a child to college is a sign of being grown up.

Privately, I think the true sign of being grown up is when you bake chocolate chip cookie dough before you eat it.

For most people, though, feeling grown up seems to have something to do with exerting authority over children. Being addressed as "Mr." or "Mrs." is a disconcerting hint that you appear grown up, but you never really feel grown up until you have children and sometimes not even then.

Still, having children of your own helps you along the road to grown-upness. After you've had several years of practice ordering your own children around, you find it easy to order other people's children around. In that respect, my daddy is the quintessential grown-up.

When we were growing up, Daddy had the chutzpah to put other people's children to work around the place. There is always a lot to be done around a country place, and Daddy saw in my big brother, Bo, and his friends a very useful labor force. Bo and Ben Trice and Skipper Royster would be hanging around the house on Saturday afternoon and Daddy would say, "All right now, you boys come on out here and help me stretch this bob wire fence and hang this gate." And they would.

My younger brother saw this happen so many times that, as a teenager, he would never invite friends over to our house to hang around on Saturday afternoons. He went to their houses, where, presumably, the fathers had not evolved into full-fledged grown-ups.

If there is a problem with youngsters today, it is that they are being raised by people like me who are uncomfortable with being authority figures. The previous generation had no such hang-ups.

My family is full of grown-ups: Not only my daddy, but my mother, too, has excellent credentials as an authority figure, and my maternal grandmother, long the matriarch of the family, was probably born a grown-up in 1895. But instead of being inspired by their example, I'm overawed. I have such respect for the grown-ups in my family that I would never presume to think of myself as one of them.

But, thanks to Katherine Bolling, I am trying.

Of course, raising my surrogate daughter, Marilynn Ware, has given me some practice being grown up. I usually think of Marilynn, who is 10 years younger than I, as a contemporary. But when I make some reference to "Auntie Mame" or the Tams or anything that happened before 1975 and she looks blank, I realize we have a generation gap.

The gap first became obvious when Marilynn and I were expecting babies at the same time. I said something about "the rabbit died" and Marilynn said, "What rabbit?"

I knew they had discontinued using the rabbit test to determine pregnancy, but I didn't realize it was that long ago.

Having impressed Marilynn with my knowledge about arcane things like prehistoric pregnancy tests, I was besieged with phone calls from her asking my advice on her symptoms and situation.

Finally I told her, "Look, I'm only one day more pregnant than you are. What makes you think I know more than you do?"

"Because you tell me how to do everything else," she said.

It was true and of course I went ahead and gave her all the advice she could possibly have wanted. I'm like my daddy, a noted advice-giver who frequently reminds people, "I don't charge anything for my advice."

I've never hesitated to give advice to friends and contemporaries, but somehow telling children what to do requires a self-concept of adultness that I haven't achieved. On the one or two occasions when I've been called upon to issue a directive to children, I've done so in a very meek way. And I've been tremendously relieved when the children have done what I asked and spared me the task of trying to be stern and grown up.

Lately, though, I have made a few tentative forays into grown-upness. My neighbor's son, who is 16 or 17, and I ride together and discuss horses and hounds as contemporaries. But recently I asserted myself as a grown-up by telling him sternly, "You ought to put those damn cigarettes away. They'll kill you."

And not too long ago I told some totally strange children to help me clean up some trash near where they were playing. They did, and I felt enormously grown up.

Maybe by the time Katherine Bolling reaches the terrible twos, I will have learned to flex my grown up, maternal muscles. However, I absolutely refuse to give up eating chocolate chip cookie dough.

CHAPTER 18

The Hard Task of Becoming
an Accomplished Young Lady

We went to hear the Richmond Sinfonia perform all six of Bach's Brandenburg Concerti recently. It was a marvelous concert of beautiful music beautifully performed.

Although I didn't realize it until I sat through the concert, those and other popular pieces from the 18th century are quite popular today. They aren't played on Q-94 or XL-102, but you've heard them more frequently than you would have guessed.

As the concert progressed, I kept expecting Ricardo Montalban to stroll on stage and give us the pitch on a Chrysler Le Baron. At other times, I expected a white-haired man in a leather chair to materialize and say, "Good evening. I'm Alistair Cook. Welcome to Masterpiece Theater. This is episode 87 of..."

Not all of the images I associate with Bach's scores come from television, I'm relieved to report.

Mostly I was reminded of Margaret Cheatham, a thin little old lady who gave piano lessons to ungrateful children in her basement in Lynchburg, Va.

Miss Cheatham -- she fit the stereotype of the spinster piano teacher --was a gentle, long-suffering soul who coaxed hundreds of pupils through scales and arpeggios from the 1940s until she retired in the 1970s.

The older I get, the more sympathy I feel for Miss Cheatham. Here was a woman who loved fine music and evidently had some talent and yet by circumstance was consigned to teach beginning piano to children who, if they were like me, didn't want to be taught.

She might have been perfectly happy, but I can't help but believe she was frustrated at having to spend her life casting pearls before swine. I imagine her turning out the light in her studio after the last lesson of the day, walking upstairs to dine alone and thinking, For this I studied eight years at the conservatory?

No such sympathetic thoughts crossed my mind between 1956 and 1968, when I was one of Miss Cheatham's students.

For my sixth birthday, my parents gave me a piano and a cowboy belt. The belt was a big success.

When I went to first grade that fall, Momma began packing me off to Miss Cheatham's two afternoons a week. In the beginning, Momma sat and waited through my 30-minute lessons, thus proving herself to be almost as long-suffering as Miss Cheatham.

Eventually, she confined her participation in my musical education to browbeating me into practicing.

Miss Cheatham's contribution, in addition to providing the actual instruction, was to provide peer pressure through a boldly displayed chart of each student's progress. Progress in various categories ("memorization," "sight-reading," "vocabulary") was measured with shiny, glue-on stars. Ten small stars added up to one large star. Gold stars were worth more than blue stars, and so on.

I didn't care a fig about playing the piano but I was intensely competitive. So I worked to keep a respectable number of stars next to my name.

Eventually, after 12 years of lessons, I learned to play the piano from a mechanical standpoint. However, I never rewarded Miss Cheatham or my parents with any indication of talent. This has always been a great disappointment to my daddy. He used to explain why I was being tortured with music lessons by describing his vision of an accomplished young lady (a vision which I in no way resembled, ever). That vision always included proficiency on the piano.

As a small child, I rebelled against practicing, but by the time I got to high school, I would put in a few hours a week without too much pressure. It helped that, after eight years, I had finally progressed beyond John Thompson's First Grade Book.

When I got to where I could play simplified versions of "real" music instead of children's learning pieces, I enjoyed the piano more. Like most piano students, I enjoyed playing pieces that I could play well, and I played them over and over during my after-dinner practice hour.

One night when I was dutifully practicing my favorite piece, "Let's Be Gay," as fast as I could hit the notes, my older brother burst from his room and hollered: "How do you expect me to learn to read Latin with Robin playing doot-doot-doot-doot a hundred times a night!?"

Another thing about being in high school that made piano lessons less painful was that performing in recitals was optional. I hated playing in recitals, mainly because I wasn't very good. As much as I disliked playing the piano, I disliked even more being showed up by Marcia Landis. Marcia Landis was pretty, popular, a good student and she effortlessly earned dozens of big gold stars for her chart. She probably kept Miss Cheatham from committing suicide, but I hated her.

So from the ninth grade on, I opted out of Miss Cheatham's recitals, which probably made her as happy as it made me. After all, I wasn't much of an advertisement for her teaching skills.

Miss Cheatham didn't fare much better with my younger brother, Cris. After five years of lessons, he still couldn't read music, even haltingly, and Miss Cheatham, who never gave up on anybody, suggested Momma and Daddy's money might be better spent on, say, tennis lessons.

This, despite the fact that Cris was the one with real musical talent. He never learned to read music because he picked everything out by ear. After being dropped from Miss Cheatham's program, Cris went on to have a brief but happy career as a drummer.

I went on to college with the idea of continuing my piano lessons, in a casual way, of course. Unfortunately for me, collegiate professors of music expect a level of accomplishment beyond being able to play "Let's Be Gay" a hundred times an hour.

So I washed out of the music department pretty quickly. My expulsion was, specifically, over my refusal to cut my fingernails short enough to play with my fingers bent at right angles. It was just the sort of untragic end to my musical career that Miss Cheatham would have predicted.

The piano sat untouched for 12 years, until May 3, 1980, when Momma bribed the organist at Court Street Methodist Church to play a few numbers for Cricket's and my wedding, which was at home.

Last year, Momma and Daddy did some remodeling to their house and wanted to dispose of the piano. They could hardly contain their mirth when I said I'd take it. "Are you going to play 'Let's Be Gay'?" Daddy asked between guffaws.

Actually, I did play it, once, just for old times' sake. Then I flipped through my old sheet music in the bench and found "Lara's Theme" from *Dr. Zhivago*, which I learned to play for Daddy in a stab at meeting his vision of an accomplished young lady.

I bought a book of nursery songs last year when I was expecting. In that one misguided moment, I saw myself playing and -- don't laugh, Daddy -- singing nursery songs with my daughter. It was about as realistic a vision as Daddy's image of an accomplished young lady.

So the piano sits here, covered with plaster dust from the construction work in the kitchen. The keyboard is open and sometimes in the middle of the night we awaken to the modernistic strains of a cat strolling down the keyboard.

And sometimes our yearling daughter stands up on tiptoes, reaches over her head and plays the keys with her tiny hands.

Now if we could only find another Miss Cheatham, the family might yet have an accomplished young lady.

CHAPTER 19

In the Privacy of Their Own Club

Women really bug me sometimes. They always want to crash all-male clubs.

Don't get me wrong. I like the unexpected pleasure of being the only woman in a roomful of men as much as the next person.

But some women aren't satisfied with that. They want to be in the club and have full access to all the facilities and all the men all the time, whether the men want them or not.

I just do not understand that attitude.

When you know you and every other woman can go be with a bunch of men any old time, it's no longer exciting. The fun is diminished because, instead of having a bunch of men with an occasional woman or two around, all you've got is a bunch of people.

Some time back, the Supreme Court ruled that men can get together and have a private pig-sticking club without any women as long as they don't have but 399 members. If they let in that 400th guy, they've got to let women in, too.

Does that make any sense to you?

This came out of a suit by some woman who was upset because the men in a private club were getting together and doing deals in their saunas and smoking rooms and she didn't have a chance to get in on them. I can see her point, but I'd like to tell her, "Honey, those fellows are going to make those deals whether you're in the smoking room or not."

Now, I'm all for men and women being together, but I think a little segregation of the sexes is good, too. It's hard for men to act civilized around women all the time, and they need the opportunity to go off by themselves and cut loose once in awhile.

The thing I like about men is that when they get together, they do what they feel like doing and they have a good time. They don't agonize about what people might think or whose feelings might get hurt. This probably explains why, although women always want to join men's clubs, you don't see any men knocking down the doors of the Junior League.

The truth is, if women knew what men did when they got together, they wouldn't want to crash their clubs.

I know, because I've been a fly on the wall at an all-male gathering.

Some years ago, a fellow named Bill asked me to go float-fishing on the James River up where it winds through the Blue Ridge Mountains. My fishing experience was, shall we say, limited, but floating down the river sounded like a fine way to spend the day.

I thought it would be just the two of us, but when we got to the put-in point, there were nine other canoes and 18 unshaven men in cutoffs and old shirts. There were also numerous coolers.

If I was surprised by the other participants in the day's adventure, they were shocked by me. They grumbled at Bill and eyed me askance. I have two brothers, so I knew my best chance for acceptance by the men was to keep a low profile and bait my own hook.

It was a beautiful day. I enjoyed the scenery, drank a beer or two, baited my own hook and caught a two-pound bass (which Bill removed from the hook).

I've always wanted to tell my fish story in print and here it is: Shortly after lunch, I hooked a big muskie about three feet from the canoe. The sight of this small whale attached to my fishing line practically within arm's reach totally undid me. The muskie swam around the canoe, jerking my rod and me to the other side and turning the canoe sideways.

Bill noticed this activity in the bow of the canoe and hollered some instructions. Since the tip of my fishing rod was bent over in the water and since the sum total of my fishing experience consisted of catching the aforementioned two-pound bass, I quickly decided to let Bill have the honor of landing this citation fish.

So I stood up in the canoe, ran to the stern and threw the rod at Bill.

"Here! You do it!" I said.

After the canoe stopped rocking, Bill began playing the muskie, or maybe the muskie played him, because he was getting whipped around just as I had been.

Some fellows in another canoe paddled over to give him a net and watch the action. The muskie broke water twice and everyone agreed it was the largest freshwater fish ever seen in the eastern half of the United States.

The largest freshwater fish in the eastern half of the United States next proceeded to snap a 20-pound test line and swim off with a hook that I had spent 10 minutes pushing a worm onto.

I was deeply relieved that Bill was holding the rod at the time. It was okay for him to lose the catch of the day but not okay for the token woman.

Hooking a whale in the upper James was the topic of conversation at the fish fry that night. Before the first bottle of bourbon was empty, that muskie had become the largest freshwater fish in the Western hemisphere.

If you can't keep a low profile with a bunch of men, the next best thing is to just miss outdoing them in some spectacular fashion.

That's the end of my fish story, but we're just getting to the reason why women shouldn't crash men's clubs.

The fish fry was held at a "camp" that some of the men owned. The "camp" was a good-sized, two story cabin with a long screened porch and a well-equipped kitchen.

I figured the men would all bring their dates and wives to the fish fry but no. Only those who floated the river that day came to dinner.

There was one exception. My dog Rally, a large, silver-and-black German shepherd who went everywhere with me except for canoes, came to the fish fry. She was quite well-received by the men, who, in light of my hooking a big fish, had decided I wasn't quite the pall on their outing they had anticipated.

Several of the men cooked up platters of fried fish and set them on a great long table on the porch. There were vegetables, cooked in some primitive, camp style. And there in the center of the table, steaming like a cannibal stewpot, was a vat of baked beans.

After a long day outdoors, we all thought it was a delicious meal.

It must have been 10 or 11 o'clock. The men had all pushed back from the table and were getting down to some serious drinking when they ran out of ice or beer or something. So a couple of them got in the car to run up to the country store.

They came back after awhile hollering and whooping and carrying the carcass of a raccoon they'd run over. They trooped the coon around the cabin, singing nonsense, and finally set him up in the half-eaten vat of baked beans.

They propped the coon up in various poses, hooting with laughter and making ridiculous jokes. Somebody stuck a cigarette in the coon's mouth and three men fell off the bench in hysterics.

Meanwhile, my dog Rally was getting excited by the smell of raccoon blood, and she put her paws on the table and barked furiously at the coon in the bean pot. This generated more excitement among the men, who egged the dog on.

The next thing you know, Rally had jumped up on the table and grabbed the coon by its neck. The climax of the evening came as this shaggy dog marched up and down the plate-strewn table growling and shaking that coon carcass while the entire float-fishing and fish-frying club staggered to its feet and gave her a lusty cheer.

Now, I'm not suggesting dogs drag dead coons up and down the table in the men's private dining room at the Metropolitan Club or the Union Club, but hey, it kind of gives you goose bumps to think about it, doesn't it, ladies?

CHAPTER 20

Blood Is Thicker Than Water
or Highway Maps

Marilynn Ware just came back from showing off her baby boy, Henry, at the Hamrick family reunion in Shelby, N.C. The Hamrick family reunion is one of those kind where they have 400 people and some of them don't even know each other.

Marilynn says it is an annual affair, which I find both astonishing and wonderful. It's astonishing to think you can get 400 people together from around the country every year. It seems like people would slack off coming because they'd think, Well, there'll be another one next year. On the other hand, I guess the reunion has become such an important tradition that no one would think of missing it.

Family reunions and other gatherings of the clan are most important to older relatives and those who live far away. The older you get and the farther away you move, the more you value the chance to get together with people who share the same raising, the same memories.

Children, on the other hand, don't have much truck with family gatherings until they've been to 25 or 30 and they've gotten to know which cousins are most apt to help devise and carry out mischievous activities. Those activities are what form the bonds between youngsters that will make them want to get together at family reunions 15 or 20 years hence.

At a Traywick family reunion last March, 13-year-old Benjamin, who had somehow escaped examination by the rest of the family for the last 12 years, got a bit testy when every single adult relative in turn expressed surprise that he was no longer a baby.

Lesson #1 in reunion etiquette: Grownups should refrain from any references to the fact that teenaged boys ever wore diapers.

What Benjamin didn't realize, of course, is that those remarks reflected a mildly shocked realization that the speaker, too, had gotten on in years. One of the tasks of attending a reunion is to find your place among the generations.

Reunions have children, parents, grandparents and often great-grandparents, but these categories are all relative. Grandparents and parents are children of somebody, too. As long as your parents are alive, you tend to think of yourself first of all as their child, even when most of your waking hours are consumed with being somebody else's parent.

It's only when you go to a reunion and see your cousins getting gray and hear about their children's going off to college that you realize a whole 'nother batch of kids has moved into the next generation.

As I looked around the room at all my cousins last March, it dawned on me that we had become the middle-aged adults who laughed and talked in my grandparents' front room while the children played in the magnolia tree in the yard.

Another important task at reunions is to recite the oral history of the family. Stories of the earliest known kin are recounted so that the newly-turned-adult generation can memorize them for their children.

As the stories are told, the family tree is traced. This always gives rise to a lengthy discussion of the difference between a third cousin and a second cousin, once removed.

(Numbered levels refer to people in the same generation, while "removed" accounts for differences in generation, e.g., the daughter of my first cousin is my first cousin once removed. My daughter and my first cousin's daughter are second cousins.)

The thing about family reunions, formally organized or not, is that you have to go now. If you don't, there will be a reunion anyway -- at Uncle Jack's funeral.

Families have to work hard at staying close despite geographical distance. Both of my parents have very strong feelings about the importance of family. We were raised on a litany of familial relationships and a series of side trips to see people who were only distantly related.

Daddy was always driving a hundred miles out of his way to see

Aunt Grace. Talk about distantly related! She was the widow of Daddy's step-uncle, John Garnett, and really no kin at all. Still, those visits meant a lot to Aunt Grace.

She was about 90 and still lived quite independently. One time when we appeared at the door, she graciously invited us in and sat us down in the parlor for a visit.

After she and Daddy had chatted about Uncle Joe and his eccentricities awhile, Daddy noticed a cloud of smoke pouring into the room from the back hall. He leaped up and said, "Aunt Grace, something's on fire!"

She got up and said, "Oh drat. I left a pan on the stove."

We followed her into the smoke-filled kitchen where, indeed, a pan was on fire. She reached for a canister of flour and dumped it on the pan, suffocating the fire instantly. The kitchen was a mess and Daddy wanted to clean it up, but Aunt Grace shooed us back into the front room to finish our visit.

Aunt Grace didn't get to talk family much and she wasn't about to let some trifle like having her house on fire interfere.

Momma, too, makes a big effort to keep up with her few living relatives, as well as many of the dead ones. When she has sought out first cousins she saw only once or twice as a child, they have been delighted at her interest.

She also has a lively relationship with librarians all over the United States as she writes to establish births, marriages and deaths of her forebears so we children can be enrolled as members of various ancestor organizations.

Thanks to Momma, I am permanently entered in the computers of several such organizations, most of whose correspondence seems to consist of offers to buy life insurance.

(Question: If we are called "descendants," why aren't our grandparents called "ascendants"?)

I often feel bad that I don't make the kind of effort Daddy did to see Aunt Grace. When I was single, I made a pilgrimage to South Carolina every summer, but it's been three or four or five years since I've been now.

Certainly I have legitimate reasons for not going. My husband's schedule, the baby, the animals, newspaper deadlines, the myriad of activities that make up the fabric of my life in Goochland, all make it hard to break away.

But I have a nagging feeling that it's really a matter of priorities. When I was growing up, we drove to South Carolina at least once a month. Momma and Daddy left the animals and took the babies and went to see the family.

Because my parents made seeing the family a top priority, I have distant cousins who are more like brothers. That blood kin and those childhood memories are powerful. When we were all together last March, there was a tremendous feeling of closeness that exemplified the word "kinship." We all shared the blood, at least laterally, of two extraordinary people, Paul and Janie Traywick.

And we all shared the memory of their house in Cameron, S.C. -- the hot bedrooms under an uninsulated roof, the climbing tree out front, the lily pond that doubled as a water hole, the cook of 40 years who told fortunes and gave us sage advice and small gifts.

I guess I shouldn't feel too bad about not going to see Uncle Tom's boys in Cope or Paul and Susan in Isle of Palms. Nowadays it's hard for me to catch up with my immediate family, much less cousins two states away. Everyone is on the go so much that I've despaired of ever seeing them all at once again.

So once a week I call and talk to their answering machines and wonder what it would be like if we all got in the car with the babies and drove to South Carolina one weekend.

CHAPTER 21

Broodmare Turned Racehorse

I t seemed like such a good idea in the beginning: riding in a steeple-chase. After all, I had one of the main prerequisites, a horse. And I enjoyed some small, but entirely false, reputation for courage. How false it was became all too clear as the spring racing season progressed and I found myself engaged in a life of constant worry punctuated by moments of sheer terror.

Some of that reputation was undoubtedly based on my willingness to ride the horse in question. The horse's name was Mele Kalikimaka, an unfortunate selection for which I confess responsibility. The name is Hawaiian for "Merry Christmas." Had I known the Hawaiian phrase, I would have called her "Thumb Your Nose," "Up Yours," or some other term indicative of her cavalier disregard for my wishes.

I bred her, raised her and, when she was two years old, broke her to ride. Then for 10 years I rode her out foxhunting. There we established our respective reputations, hers for excessive enthusiasm and mine for white knuckles. I don't know whether she thought she was one of the hounds or what, but she motor-crossed through the woods without any respect for hunt field etiquette or the proximity of tree limbs to trails. We came home from every hunt with Mele snorting flames and me battered and bloody. Once, in desperation, I gave her a tranquilizer. As it happened I gave her a bit too much, and she spent the day staggering around the woods leaning on trees. After that I went back to working without a net.

Possibly the highlight of her hunting career was the day she dove off an eight-foot bank into the confluence of Beaverdam and Courthouse creeks. The temperature was about 20 degrees. The water was exactly waist-deep. (I understand they pay stunt actors lots of money for that sort of thing.)

When I got home, dripping water where I didn't have icicles, my husband said, "And you want to breed that mare and get another one like her?"

We did breed her, and the whole experience was about as pleasant as diving into Beaverdam Creek in the wintertime. Although Mele was agreeable enough when it came to conceiving the foal, she absolutely refused to give birth. Every night for weeks, I got up at two-hour intervals to see if parturition was imminent. Mele would give me a disgusted look as I stumbled into her stall in my nightgown and goose down jacket. No doubt she thought: Here comes that pervert with a flashlight to look at my private parts again.

Mele did finally foal, just shy of a Guinness record for gestation, but it took me and two strong men to bring the colt safely into the world. Mele timed the blessed event to occur just as our house guests and their four children arrived for the weekend. The mare's initial response was to refuse to let the colt nurse, thus requiring another all-nighter during which I held the mare while my husband plugged the foal into her milk bag.

Mele relented eventually, but she was never what you'd call a doting mother. She always had a look of stoic resignation on her face when the colt was nursing. By the time he was five or six weeks old, Mele was begging me to put him in a day care center and let her go back to work. When the colt was five months old, we put him in the care of Uncle Bomber, a kind gelding. Mele cheerfully returned to foxhunting in hopes of getting her figure back.

Motherhood hadn't mellowed her appreciably. All it had done was to make her brazenly flirtatious. At every opportunity, she would sidle up to some poor eunuch of a gelding, arch her neck provocatively and emit a husky, come-hither whinny.

Clearly, I had to find something for this horse to do. I took inventory of her talents: She liked to run. Racing seemed like the answer, but they don't let 13-year-old broodmares run in the Kentucky Derby. She was a wonderful, cat-like jumper. Steeplechasing then. The only drawback there was my secret desire to live into old age.

Mele had another attribute that was important for racing: She was tough as nails. In 10 seasons of foxhunting, including the year she was in foal, she'd never suffered more than a stone bruise. She stayed outside in her natural coat all the time, except a few nights in the winter. She never had a cough or a cold, never tied up, never got tired. She really belied the Thoroughbred image of delicacy.

I don't know when the idea of racing over fences took hold. It might have been the day we were hunting and Mele, in the course of rocketing across country, nearly stepped on the fox. Or it might have been the day of our club's pair races, when Mele and I finished three whole minutes ahead of our partner. Anyway, around Christmas, I started galloping her on a semi-regular basis. I'd been whipping-in off her all fall, and she was hunting fit.

One day when the ground was frozen tight, I drove the pickup truck around the perimeter of all the neighborhood fields, so I'd know how far I was galloping. My training program, such as it was, evolved from bits and snatches of racing knowledge I'd picked up over the years, plus what I could glean from chance encounters with cognoscenti. I took to grilling everyone who'd ever even seen a race over fences. I read books on training methods and somehow came up with a vague plan of action, the main feature of which was *we'll see how it goes.* Since I have a life outside of horses, the training program had to be, above all, flexible.

At first it was great fun. Then as winter set in and I took a temporary job, I began to question my commitment to this supposedly fun undertaking. Usually, the sun was setting when I got home from work. It was so dark when I rode most of the time that I couldn't see my watch to time Mele. I just punched the stopwatch buttons and read the time when we got back to the barn. Out of necessity, I developed a feel for pace.

The weather never interfered, though. When I had the opportunity to ride, I rode. We went out in snow, in rain (lots of rain), in bitter cold, in dark of night --sometimes all four. By the time race day rolled around, we were prepared for anything except a sunny day.

There were bright spots. I like being outdoors in winter because you see so much wildlife. We shared the fields with deer who came out to feed at night, sometimes in herds of 10 or more. They would watch us with interest, spooking and flipping their white flags only if we rode straight toward them. Hawks and owls flew across the wooded path as we hacked home in the twilight. And Canada geese cheered us with their honking overhead.

It turned out there was more to this project than simply galloping the horse as often as possible. For one thing, I had to find out when, where and under what conditions an appropriate race would be held.

My original plan was to ride in some old-fashioned point-to-points and gradually work up to a heads-up race. I sent off for the condition book for the Virginia point-to-point circuit, which turned out to have zippo about old-fashioned races. But lo! there was a race for beginners at Casanova on Feb. 22. "Foxhunters Race -- about 2 1/4 miles over fair hunting country." (I found out later that means timber.) "For riders and horses who are not yet ready for regular point-to-point competition."

I could ride in my hunting attire, rather than silks, but I had to have certain equipment. The overgirth I bought was way too big for my little 15.1-hand mare, so I took it to a shoe shop and had them take a tuck in it. The biggest problem was figuring out how to make the minimum weight of 160 pounds. Dressed, I weighed 132 pounds, so the search was on for a big heavy saddle with big heavy stirrups. I also stepped up my consumption of cream puffs and ice cream. By race day, I needed only three pounds of artificial weight.

Ten days or so before the race, I began to get nervous. Periodic phone calls to interested parties kept me going. I asked Peter Winants, the editor of "The Chronicle of the Horse," who had never seen me in person, much less on a horse, if he thought I could handle this. He cheerfully encouraged me, promising to walk the course with me before the race.

One day I ran into two race riders and nervously begged for guidance. They went through a checklist and I was able to answer affirmatively until they started talking about jumping.

"You know you have to stand back at the fences when you're jumping at speed," they said. "If you leave the ground too close, you'll be dead."

Yes, I knew that.

"Does your horse know that? Have you schooled her?"

I suppose the reason I didn't think to put schooling in my training program was that Mele was such a good jumper. Nevertheless, to calm my nerves, we went out one afternoon and schooled over a little chicken coop with a rail on top. Not exactly your regulation National Steeplechase Association fence. Mele thought barreling into the fence at top speed and leaving the ground from downtown was great fun, and I rode home confident we could survive a timber race.

As I look back now, from the still-modest vantage point of four races' experience, I'm horrified at my naiveté. God really does look out for fools and idiots, and Mele looked out for me.

One moment of panic spoiled an otherwise calm pre-race week. Mele and the other horses were standing outside up to their fetlocks in mud while I was bedding the stalls. Suddenly I noticed Mele favoring her right front foot.

"She's lame!" I shrieked to my husband. "Look at her! She's lame!"

We got her in the barn and I asked Cricket to jog her in the aisle way. "See! She's lame!"

"She's not lame," he said. He was right. She wasn't lame.

Race day dawned cold and gray. We bundled up and began the two-hour drive to Warrenton. A small, hardy band of supporters met us at the course. We'd had a lot of rain and the footing was bound to be slow. My only fear was that the turf would be chewed up and sloppy by the time the seventh race went off. When we drove in the gate and promptly got stuck in the mud, it seemed like a bad omen. A big tractor had to pull us into line with the vans.

As Peter Winants and I walked the course, it started to snow. Big flakes. Torrents of flakes. In 15 minutes, it was snowing like a bandit. By the time my race went off two hours later, there were two inches of snow on the ground. Cricket asked if I really wanted to go ahead with this. I had my doubts, but, after all, we were there, and we'd worked two months to get there.

By the time we rode out on the track, the fences were all covered with snow. Horses running on the backstretch appeared as mere shadows. I trotted Mele up to the first fence to give her a look and came back for the start. She felt good. I figured we could canter around the course and survive.

But, of course, that was not the way it turned out.

We got off first at the start, but I went slowly and let two men pass me before the first fence. There was another woman in the race, but I never saw her after we warmed up. In fact, I hardly saw anything after we warmed up. The snow completely covered my goggles in the first hundred yards, and I had to rip them off before the first fence. Then I was blinded by snow cutting my face. Mele, meanwhile, took the snow, the soft footing and the first fence in stride.

By the beginning of the second round, the two men were about 15 lengths ahead of me. I decided I'd better start cutting that down and chirped to Mele on the flat between fences. Then one of the men fell at a fence. We had room to go around and I had time to note that it didn't look like a bad fall.

By the beginning of the third and final round, Mele was within striking distance of the leader, a man on a big chestnut gelding. We made a move on the inside, and he pulled over in front of me. He'd been weaving around a lot, even going on the wide side of one of the brush fences, and I was wary of his riding. I was still anxious to have my own pocket of space, so I went to the outside. He looked back and pulled over in front of me again.

I believe it was at that point that I quit worrying about survival and decided I wanted to win. After safely negotiating the next fence, I gunned Mele up beside him and hollered: "Move over, you person of questionable parentage!" or something like that. Later I was embarrassed, but at the time I was furious.

By then the horses were steaming into the next-to-last fence. He tried to ride me wide of the fence, but Mele held her ground as I offered him more advice on where to ride.

Even now when I think about jumping that fence from God knows how far away, I get a stomach ache. Mele made an enormous leap, picking up three strides and the lead. My friends said later that the announcer was screaming, "Now it's Mele Kalikimaka! Mele Kalikimaka! That means Merry Christmas in Hawaiian, and look at her in the snow!"

It would be nice to say this heroic effort led to the winner's circle, but alas, the big gelding came up on the inside and took the lead back at the final fence. I went wide on the last turn and we had to chase him down the stretch. Mele came on gamely, gaining every stride, but a photo of the finish showed us half a length shy of the win.

It was, quite simply, the most exciting thing I've ever done. The adrenalin surge that last half-mile put me on a high for three days. Mele and I were both bouncing off the walls until about Tuesday. Once we recovered, I knew we had to try that again. I wanted a rematch with the chestnut gelding, but most of all, I wanted to jump those last two fences again, to feel that rush of risk as I asked and my horse gave her utmost.

I decided to enter some ladies races, get some more experience and aim for the foxhunters race at Rappahannock on April 27, the last day of the season. The ladies races are generally the fastest timber races of the day, I learned, as the women carry only 145 pounds. Once considered easy races on the circuit, they now attract professional riders and top horses. We would be outclassed, but my goal was, first of all, to finish, and second, to gain some experience riding over fences at speed.

I groped my way through the spring, pitting my non-existent training skills against the professionally-trained horses and riders on the circuit. At Warrenton in a three-mile race, the heat and soft footing took their toll on Mele. She ran well for two miles, then tired. I took encouragement from the fact that we didn't fall and we didn't finish last.

I learned from Warrenton that Mele wasn't fit. Incredible as it must have seemed to the professionals, I was only riding her every other day. After that, we began to train more earnestly. Mele seemed to thrive on the training. She ate well and, although she was working harder than she had ever worked in her life, she actually put on weight. Although she had always been semi-wild in the hunting field, she had a marvelous calmness about racing. In the paddock at each race while the other horses were prancing around, Mele wanted to graze. I always had to pull the grass out of her mouth so she wouldn't choke during the race. And she paraded onto the track with loose reins. Hi, folks. But when the starter dropped the flag, she was short-coupled and long gone.

Cricket and I had fun at the races, too. Several friends came to cheer us on and we made new friends of the regular participants. People noticed the little mare with the funny name who was such a terrific jumper. Although I was always a babbling idiot on race day, I managed to remember the names of some of the officials and others who explained the rules and offered encouragement.

At Old Dominion, Mele ran her best race to date in a chilly rain. The ladies races usually had lots of entries, and I was wary of being in a crowd at the first fence, so I always hung back at the start. But at Old Dominion, several riders announced at the start that they were on green horses. Furthermore, the fences at Old Dominion seemed bigger and I got spooked. I managed to get out in front of the green horses at the start, but I was afraid to let Mele go as fast as the leaders. We seemed to meet every fence wrong, and after a near-disaster, I heard the voice of a race rider I knew saying *You can't check them at the fences, you've got to send them on.*

So on the second round, we picked up speed and I drove Mele into each fence. She stood back and made a huge leap over every fence, as I grabbed her mane just to stay on. She finished fifth, but I knew she could have done much better if I'd asked her to run sooner. I couldn't pull her up at the end, so I knew then that she was finally fit.

The last three weeks before the foxhunter race at Rappahannock were the most miserable time of my life. Everyone expected me to win and everyone told me to quit holding Mele back. I was trying to learn to ride with my irons shorter, and I must have spent three hours every day agonizing over it: three holes shorter? four holes shorter? five? I practiced jumping shorter, but Mele was bored and wouldn't stand back, which made me worry all the more. My stomach was in knots all the time. Between the daily galloping and my inability to eat, I lost five pounds, which was a lot for me.

I drove to Rappahannock and walked the course on Thursday before the race on Sunday, hoping that would calm my nerves. It didn't. The course is on the side of a mountain, and on a pretty April afternoon, nothing could have been lovelier. There is this hill between the second and third fences that I'd been hearing about. You jump the first two fences going uphill, then you pass a flag and come rolling off the mountain to a jump at the bottom. It didn't look too bad from the bottom, but when I climbed to the top I saw what everybody was talking about. It was like coming over the top of the old roller coaster at Ocean View Amusement Park. I went home and dreamed about that hill for three days.

On Friday I blew Mele out up a couple of steep hills to tune her up for Sunday. She came back in fine form, but when I got off at the barn, I was horrified to see blood all over her right front leg. She had run a stick or stob up the inside of her leg between the bone and the tendon, and it wouldn't stop bleeding. Numbly, I washed her leg and put a pressure bandage on to stop the bleeding. Mele walked calmly around the paddock without a trance of a limp, but I had a new rock in my stomach.

That evening she was still sound, although the wound started to bleed again when I removed the bandage. It was the sort of wound that would heal itself, especially on a tough old bird like Mele, but how would she feel in 48 hours? My biggest fear was that it would close up, swell and make her sore. So I began hosing her leg with cold water to keep the heat down, then wrapping it with towels soaked in hot Epsom salts to keep the wound open and draining.

By Saturday she was doing well, but I was sick to my stomach. I went from my bed to the bathroom to the barn and back again all day. I had gotten the list of entries for the races. Mele could win her race, but it would mean riding hard for two miles. No tip-toeing off the side of the mountain. To win, I'd have to let her run down that big hill and hope for the best when we got to the fence at the bottom. I didn't think I had the guts to do it. I kept hoping Mele's leg would get sore, which would give me a perfect out.

Saturday night I was feeling better and Mele's wound looked like a scratch. About 9:30 p.m., I finished working around the barn and turned the horses out for the night. Cricket was hitching up the trailer and the gate was open. Mele and her buddy went out--and down the road!

They went a mile down the road to another farm and hung over the fence to talk to the horses there. I was jogging along behind with a flashlight and the dogs. Mele was in high spirits and had no intention of going home. The neighbors and I spent an hour trying to catch her before she gave up and turned herself in to Cricket.

Sunday morning Mele was still sound, so we decided to go to the races. It was a beautiful day for spectators but mighty hot for running horses.

That, coupled with our myriad of other excuses, made me fairly calm.

I arranged to borrow a weight pad and 15 pounds of lead to get me up to 160 pounds. I never knew where to put the weight pad or the number cloth: number cloth, weight pad, saddle pad? Or saddle pad, number cloth, weight pad? Somehow, I got it all on Mele in what looked like a comfortable arrangement and we went to the paddock.

There I saw two of the longest-legged horses I'd ever seen in my life. They looked like giraffes. They made Mele look like a pony. One of them was a regular winner of old-fashioned races and the other, a 17-hand brown horse, belonged to a family of professional horsemen. I got on and rode to my doom.

As soon as the starter dropped the flag, though, the competitive urge took over. Mele jumped out to the lead and when I heard hoofbeats close behind, I reached down and got another gear. Mele led the way up hill and over the first two fences, but the brown horse was breathing down her neck. His rider had said as we rode to the post that he planned to take the lead and set a fast pace, but he never could head Mele.

He finally came up beside us after the second fence, and Mele had to hold her ground to keep from being pushed outside the flag at the top of the mountain. She made a tight turn around the flag, rocketed down the roller coaster hill and sailed over the fence at the bottom. The brown horse disappeared from view and we never saw or heard him again.

Mele had started her stretch run with nine fences and a mile and a half to go! Spectators nodded and said she'd never maintain that pace up those hills in that heat for two miles. I forced myself to let her run and jump. I just steered her toward the fences and she thundered around the course so fast the wind tore tears from my eyes. It was a thrilling feeling.

When she came across the finish line 15 or 20 lengths ahead of the others, she still wanted to run. I was grinning like a 'possum, I was so proud of that little mare! After 13 years, she'd finally found her niche.

Cricket ran up to hold her so that I could unsaddle her and weigh in. As he took the reins, he asked anxiously, "Do you still have your weight pad?"

Just then, one of the outriders rode up carrying my weight pad and number cloth, which had worked loose and come off at the beginning of the second mile. Needless to say, I weighed in 15 pounds light and Mele was disqualified. It was a great disappointment to our friends, new and old, who had watched our progress during the season. Half a dozen riders, trainers or officials came up to me afterwards and said, "Please let me tack up your horse next time."

Gladly.

Everyone else was more upset than I. I was embarrassed that inexperience got us in the end, and I was sorry Mele wouldn't get the credit for her win. But I was too excited over Mele's magnificent performance to feel bad.

In my misery the day before the race, I told my parents this would be our last race.

But I lied.

Editor's note: Mele pulled a suspensory ligament while training for the next season and never raced again. Years later, however, Mele's son vindicated her racing "career" with a win in his one and only start over jumps.

CHAPTER 22

We Could Always Call Her 'Junior'

We have a seven-month-old daughter who goes with me just about everywhere. She's an engaging child and, naturally, people will chuck her under the chin and ask, "What's her name?"

There's always a strange pause while I try to think, *What is her name?*

It's not that I can't remember, exactly, it's that I'm not sure what to call her. Her given name is Katherine Bolling. I wanted to call her Bolling, which I think is both unusual and pretty, but it wouldn't stick. Her father calls her Katherine because he believes it's against the law to call a child by her middle name. My compromise is to call her Katie most of the time. When I'm tickling her, though, I call her Little Fat Person, and when she's torturing the dogs, I call her Katie Bo.

So it gives me pause when someone casually asks, "What's her name?"

Naming a baby is an extraordinarily tricky undertaking. It's so fraught with controversy that the name you select should never be discussed with friends or family in advance of the child's birth, when the name is simply and firmly announced.

There are two kinds of people in the world: those who think parents ought to use family names exclusively, regardless of the burden this places on the child, and those who think parents ought to pick euphonic names out of the air, regardless of the burden this places on the child. No matter which side you're on, everyone you talk to will be on the other side.

I'm of the family-names-only school of thought, and I spent many hours poring over the family trees looking for a couple of complementary twigs. My husband, Cricket, rejected every female name on his side right off the bat and there aren't many on my side (I have an aunt named Bruce, for example), so the pickings were slim. My mother said not to use her name, Flo, because it sounds like a dance hall girl. About the only thing left was Sophronia Othneil, but that would have given our daughter the initials SOW, among other problems.

There are worse names than Sophronia Othneil Williams, but not many.

We have always found great entertainment value in the names of my daddy's neighbors in Cameron, the small South Carolina village where he was raised. My brother Cris says his favorite is Nonnie Ducky Smoak, which is a woman's name. I've always been partial to Fairey Prickett, which is a man's name.

Daddy says the Danzler family had the best names. They had three sons, Cloyce, Ottice and Hezekiah, and two daughters, Norene and Clorene.

Momma says you can't talk about anybody in Cameron until you've dealt with my daddy, whose name is Heber Venable Bainbridge Traywick. Like most adults, he's resigned to his name now, but childhood was rough, even with friends named Jehu Alonzo Smoak and Hezzie Danzler.

"When I was, oh, about 11," Daddy recalled, "they published a book of South Carolina families, and they had me in there as 'Helen.' It just ruined my life. 'Heber' was bad enough."

If he felt that way, why do you suppose I have a brother named Heber Venable Bainbridge Traywick, Jr.?

My granddaddy, whose name was Asa Paul Traywick, had a grand time naming babies. He named all five of his own without any help, even from my grandmother. (Since he was responsible for Heber Venable Bainbridge, maybe he needed some help.)

He was the village doctor and he delivered every baby born in Calhoun County in the first half of the 20th century. He also named a good many of them, mostly after himself.

Granddaddy and the proud new father would be celebrating the happy occasion out on the front porch and the father would say, "Well, Doc, what do you think we ought to name him?"

Granddaddy would look thoughtful and say, "How about 'Paul'?"

There was an amazing number of Pauls in Calhoun County.

One day he delivered the ninth or 10th child in a family. Granddaddy and the father, Burley Wiles, were sitting on the porch, and Burley said, "Well, Doc, what do you think we ought to name him?"

"How about 'Paul'?" Granddaddy said on cue.

"We already got a 'Paul,'" Burley said.

Granddaddy thought over all of Burley Wiles' children's names. "Have you got a Burley Junior?"

Burley Wiles' face lit up. "No sir, Doc. Burley Junior. That's great!"

Some time later Granddaddy went back to check on the new baby. "How's Burley Junior doing?" he asked.

And Burley Wiles said, "He's doing fine, Doc, but we didn't name him Burley Junior. We named him Harvey Junior. Harvey Junior Wiles."

Naming pets is so much easier than naming children. The difficulty in naming a child is that you have to name her the first time you lay eyes on her, or sooner. With a pet, you can take two or three months to get to know its personality first.

For instance, we have a cat named Fat Squeak, after his most salient characteristics.

We have another cat, a feisty little female who, when she showed up on our doorstep, was a scrawny, street-wise, adolescent mother-to-be. Her name is Welfare.

We took a long time naming our current German shepherd. We had a lot of advice from Stuart Johnson, who has a special fondness for German shepherds. Stuart reminded us repeatedly of the necessity of giving a German shepherd a proper name.

"Shepherds are noble dogs and it's important to give them noble names. A German shepherd hates to be laughed at, and you don't want to give one a ridiculous name. They know."

Puppies, even German shepherd puppies, are not noted for their noble instincts. As a puppy, our shepherd was especially un-noble. Her favorite pastimes were leaping onto the hoods of automobiles and bringing home unmentionables from the neighbor's clothesline. She had a screw loose somewhere and a corkscrew tail, so we named her Pigtail. Stuart was horrified.

Our other dog, whose name should be Barkie, is named Blackie. He is absolutely worthless and doesn't respond to any name or command. He thinks his name means "play dead." That's because the only time we call him is to put him outside, where he doesn't want to be. If he happens to get off the sofa and wander around the house, I'll say, "Blackie..." Before I can get to the part about going outside, he hits the floor like he's been shot. Then I have to pick him up like a sack of meal and drag him to the door.

When we had a colt three years ago, I had a wonderful time thinking up names. The sire and dam had impossible names to work with (Mele Kalikimaka and Hell or Heaven), so I went in another direction.

I wanted to call the colt Sailor, but I needed some justification. I remembered hearing my brother, Bo, who is quite a student of the Civil War, talk about the battle of Saylers Creek. It seemed to me our great-grandfather had been captured there. That would make a good name for the colt, a good name with a good story.

One day I told Bo about naming the colt, expecting him to be pleased. He nodded and, after some hesitation, said, "Great-granddaddy wasn't captured at the battle of Saylers Creek. He was captured at the battle of Cedar Creek."

Rats. Oh well, Cedar Creek sounded pretty good.

Then Bo nodded again. "Actually, it wasn't the battle of Cedar Creek. It was near there, but it was called the battle of Fisher's Hill."

So the colt's name is Saylers Creek and I just lie about it.

CHAPTER 23

How I Was Cured of Being a Health Nut

I'm convinced that walking is the best form of exercise there is. It's easy, painless and good for your brain as well as your body. I've been doing a lot of walking lately, as well as other exercise, in an effort to recover from the ravages of having a baby at my advanced age.

Several people have suggested that I join an exercise class or a health club, but I'm not into organized calisthenics. I figure anybody who lives in the country and takes care of three horses doesn't need a health spa.

I tried a health club one time and it just wasn't for me. I was working a desk job at the time and felt out of shape. Remembering what a glowing specimen of good health I had been when I worked on a farm and tossed bales of hay around all day, I decided to make a stab at regaining, if not my youth, at least some muscle tone. Despite my contention that "indoor exercise" is a contradiction in terms, I figured I'd do what city folks do and go to the spa.

As it turned out, my contention was wrong. You really can get a lot of exercise at one of those places, more than you want, if you really try. I could hardly wait for my trial week to be over so I could quit torturing myself.

In retrospect, though, it was the culture shock that did me in. I didn't have the right wardrobe, mental attitude or marital status.

Dropping by a spa one afternoon to investigate prices, I was greeted by two smiley faces. One was the big yellow round symbol that means "have a happy day," and the other belonged to the golden-haired spa manager, who had a salon suntan to go with his spa muscles.

Smiley asked me to sign in, being sure to include my age and marital status (photo not required). I glanced down the list of ages (17, 20, 19, 18, etc.) and the marital status column (singlesinglesingle) and had the first of many misgivings about this project.

Before I could say "Arnold Schwarzenegger," Smiley had me signed up for a free week. Blondie, a tiny high school student, bounced in and took me on a tour of the facilities. We went through a glass door into the workout area, a room with mirrors on three walls and a collection of sinister-looking machines. Prancing through the purple shag carpet, Blondie rattled off the names and functions of the shiny steel racks, wheels, weights and torture beds.

Marquis de Sade, eat your heart out.

Then she then led me into her office where she briskly took my measurements so we could set up goals. After checking off "sedentary" and "lack of exercise," she asked, "If something happens, which hospital would you rather go to?"

Most of the goals we set were modest: losing a couple of pounds, dropping a half an inch from my thighs. Even the idea of losing nearly two inches from my waist didn't seem impossible, but I really didn't think I could take four and a half inches off my abdomen without plastic surgery. Blondie insisted I could lose around my ankles and gain in my bust, but I pointed out that my ankles were already too thin and, at my age, my bust wasn't likely to grow unless I started nursing a baby again.

The next day I returned to begin the regimen Blondie had devised for me. Clad in eminently sensible track shorts and a t-shirt, I nonetheless felt dowdy in the midst of the young nymphs in variegated leotards and tights who were twisting and firming and lifting and losing without so much as a heavy breath or a bead of salty moisture.

I did an exhaustive tour of the "resistance equipment" before I found the "beautiful posture bar," which allowed me to stand in a normal position and fake exercise while watching the other patrons.

Smiley came into the women's exercise room and struck up a conversation, giving me a chance to catch my breath. I made some comment about the muscle-bound men we could see entering their exercise room.

Smiley, sucking in his stomach, protested. He went into a long explanation of how much he'd gained since he started working out ("Muscle weighs more than fat," I was told for the 20th time) and how some of the spa members were in competition.

"I want to start competing this fall. I can bench-press 350 pounds now and I'd like to be able to bench 400 by November."

"How much do you have to be able to bench to compete?" I asked.

"They don't lift weights in competition," he told me patiently. "They pose."

Before I could learn more, Blondie dragged me off to exercise class. I never could get the choreography straight. The instructor would say, "Twist to the left twice then touch your toes and stretch, reach for the ceiling, bend your back right and left 10 times. Ready? Go!"

Everybody would leap into rhythmic action except me. They went through the routines so fast that I was still jumping my jack when they were touching their noses to their toes.

Panting, I dragged my blenderized body into the locker room to change into my bathing suit and hit the whirlpool. Luxuriating in the heated whirlpool turned out to be the saving grace of my experiment in health, although the fact that the whirlpool was coed made me somewhat uncomfortable.

You have that elevator etiquette problem in a whirlpool: Where do you look when you're in a tiny pool full of strangers with practically nothing on, leaning against the wall with a jet of water poking you in the side? Still, the whirlpool turned out to be the site of some interesting encounters.

My first day in the whirlpool, the Marlboro Man joined me and opened with, "Come here often?" followed by a first-name-only introduction. After a coy exchange on the subject of employment (he sold scuba equipment in the summer and "hung around" in the winter), he noticed my wedding rings and gasped, "Are you married?"

When I confessed that I was, he said, "How long have you been married?" in an indignant tone that implied I had somehow acquired a husband in the five minutes since we'd met.

One day while staring at the poolside statuary in my best elevator style, I overheard this exchange between Adonis of the Bulging Biceps and a gum-chewing blonde bombshell in a slinky purple suit.

Adonis of the B.B. opened with: "Did you work out hard?"

She smiled and nodded.

Next, he indicated her heavy eye makeup and asked, "Is that smudge-proof?"

"No, why? Is it smudged?" she asked in alarm.

He assured her that it wasn't. "You must not have sweated much," he said.

She insisted that she did.

I suppose I should have been flattered when one of the fellows flirted with me, but in fact I was too surprised by his approach to feel complimented. My last day, as I was forcing myself through the final exhaustive round on the machines, Smiley came by to offer more advice on how to stretch my muscles into steely strands of fiber. Tearing himself away as he saw his boss come in, Smiley threw me a flirtatious smile and said, "I saw you come in in that dress. You looked good. I really like that color."

The dress was gray.

CHAPTER 24

The Secret of Winter Is Its Little Pleasures

This is my time of year. It's coming on winter and I'm ready and waiting.

Summer, thank goodness, is finally over, a bitter memory of dry ground, humid air and hideous temperatures. What I hate about summer is you feel worse as the day goes on, as opposed to winter, when you get up in the cold and you get more comfortable as the day goes on.

That doesn't mean I relish being cold. You have to dress for winter to enjoy it, which means goose down and gloves outdoors and long handles indoors and out. We keep the house fairly cool, and the baby and I wear long johns all winter.

I love long underwear. One winter when I was working downtown and hemlines were nearly ankle length, I wore long underwear to work every day. All I had to do was hike the legs up a little bit so they didn't show.

I was talking to Kay Higgins one day about doing something outside in January and she complained about being cold. Turned out she was wearing slacks, no long johns and a car coat. I reckon she was cold. You've got to put on some clothes to go outside in January.

If you dress right, you can be warm as toast and enjoy a wonderful season.

It's invigorating to go outside in the cold and DO something, then come in for hot chocolate or tea. I get a little stir crazy staying in the house all day long. Not only does it make me feel good physically to go outside and do something in the cold, it makes me feel virtuous.

I discovered the secret of winter in 1972, when I spent a year working on a horse farm in Orange County. We exercised a barn full of racehorses in all weather all winter, and we took care of two barns full of horses. Ever since then I've viewed the approach of winter with excitement.

When you're outside in all weather, little things give you such pleasure. A hot cup of coffee tastes like the nectar of the gods, sort of like a cold beer tastes after you've mowed the lawn on a hot day. There's great pleasure and satisfaction in burning that last pile of leaves or tidying the garden for a long winter's sleep.

Those odd, unexpectedly mild days are a treat, too. On a recent such day, several friends and neighbors gathered to fell a big oak tree that had died and cut it up for firewood. The women and children stood on the hill and watched as the men sawed and chopped and wedged the reluctant tree, aiming it for a landing in the clear.

When the tree was standing on a splinter, Mike Caskie administered the final cut. We all watched in awe as the tree swayed and fell with a limb-shattering crash directly across our pasture fence. The tree fell away from all the spectators but also away from the designated crash site.

The logs will burn just as brightly, though. Perhaps more so, accompanied by the retelling of the felling of the tree.

Chief of winter's pleasures for me is the opportunity to see so much wildlife in the open woods. I nearly always see an owl when I ride through the woods -- sailing almost sinisterly between the trees without flapping his wings. Just off the trail, chipmunks and little birds rustle in the leaves for nuts and berries.

And then my horse starts as a white-tailed deer explodes from underfoot and bounds away.

Wild creatures, deer especially, often seem half-tame. Recently a buck stood up about 30 feet from the trail where I was riding. I paused for the pleasure of being so close to a wild thing, my horse and I scarcely breathing as we watched quietly. The deer traded stare for stare. After a minute or two, he walked off with great composure and dignity. When he was gone, we continued on our way.

It's amazing how puffed up you can get when a denizen of the woods accepts your presence in his living room. An encounter like that always makes me feel like I'm a skilled woodsman, knowledgeable in the ways of wildlife. But the sad truth is that the land is becoming so heavily developed, the animals have become accustomed to seeing people poking around their dens and game trails.

Another of the little pleasures that arrive with winter and the holidays is contentment. It gives me a contented feeling to look out the window and know that our stable will be a cosy shelter for the horses and cats when the bitter weather arrives. There's a bin full of wood shavings for bedding the stalls, and our zeppelin cat, Fat Squeak, has already made a nest behind the half-wall in front. From where I sit, I can see the top of his black and white face peeping over the wall.

Next to the shavings bin are tiers of sweet-smelling hay to keep the horses fat until the spring grass comes in. The other cats have made nests in the hay and they come in the house carrying the soft, sweet smell of summer grass.

Yesterday I dug the dusty, dented water heater out of the cupboard and put it in the trough at the barn. I'll have to drain the trough in the front field or keep an ax handle nearby to break the ice.

Last week I bought a new 50-pound salt block and put it in the field next to the stable. The deer who live in our woods use it as freely as the horses. Many a night I've gone to the barn and startled deer at the salt lick.

One night recently I came upon a deer and a red fox there in the light, not 100 feet from the barn. They saw me at the gate and, since I came no closer, they returned to their browsing. The neighbor's barking dogs didn't drive them away, but our own dogs did. They must know which dogs are penned.

Morning trips to the barn are equally as rewarding. If you get out at just the right time in the morning, the big barn at Thorncliff, on a hillside a mile or so west of here, will be glowing pink and gold while our barn is still in shadow.

Our stable overlooks a pond on the State Farm that is a popular rest stop for migrating Canada geese. Usually I hear their haunting call overhead before I see five or six birds in formation. They are black silhouettes until they glide through a shaft of sunlight and suddenly flash gold.

We have a lot of kestrels, too, those beautifully colored small hawks that George Mitchell cusses because they snatch songbirds right off his feeders.

Last week as I drove down the steep hill on Dover Road that overlooks the river and the Sabot Hill bottomland, a sky-filling flock of starlings rose up in front of me. The sun sparkled on hundreds of black wings and, as the swarm wheeled and sailed across my windshield, it looked like a silver scarf waving in the wind.

The sight of a solitary red-tailed hawk cruising a likely luncheon site is just as impressive.

Winter is the best time for star-gazing, too. The summer haze is gone and the crisp air is so clear the stars seem just beyond the bare treetops. As with watching wildlife, the visibility is greater after the leaves fall.

In the summer, we content ourselves with sitting on the porch and looking at Scorpio and Sagittarius in the southern sky. But this time of year, it seems we can see the whole sky: Orion's belt and Taurus in the east, the brilliant star Vega burning in the west, the ursine brothers, big dipper and little, in the north, and a panoply of lesser-known stars all across the southern sky.

Enough of this office work. I'm going to take the baby and see what animals are waiting for us in the woods.

CHAPTER 25

The Facts of Gender, or, Indulging Imelda

I melda Marcos, wife of the deposed Philippine president, said once that her name would go down in the dictionary as a synonym for the superlative form of "extravagant."

She and her husband, who were charged with ripping off the Filipino treasury to the tune of ultra-multi-millions, will undoubtedly go down in the Guinness Book of Records, too. Not since Louis XVI has a head of state expended so much of his country's wealth on so many frivolities.

Chief among Ferdinand Marcos' frivolities was indulging Imelda. Imelda's name has already entered the language (if not the dictionary), but not as the definition for general extravagance. "Imelda" is synonymous with a specific form of extravagance: shoes.

Think about it. What do you remember most about the Philippine people overrunning the Marcoses' palace? --That photograph of Imelda's 3,000 pairs of shoes, what else?

News that Imelda Marcos had 3,000 pairs of shoes epitomized the ridiculousness of her self-indulgence, but it made American women everywhere look good by comparison.

My husband, Cricket, has been known to comment on the fact that I have what he considers to be an excessive number of shoes. His comments on my footgear inevitably lead to a discussion of what, exactly, is the "right" number of shoes for a person to own.

We begin by agreeing that 3,000 is too many. Even if you changed shoes six times a day, it would take almost two years to wear every pair once. Likewise, 2,000 is too many, and really, so is 1,000.

And I think, for most people, 500 pairs of shoes is probably more than is necessary. So Cricket and I are in agreement that far. The problem comes when he wants to apply zero-based budgeting to my shoe wardrobe. He thinks that I should establish some base, fixed number, like four, as the optimum size of my shoe collection.

I, on the other hand, think the optimum number of shoes should be based on what clothes you have to wear them with and how often you can get to the Craddock-Terry shoe factory outlet in Lynchburg.

It was ever thus, mainly because women are different from men.

Look in the closets of every married couple you know and this is what you will find: She has a minimum of 50 pairs of shoes. He has two, one pair of dress shoes and one pair of work shoes.

The number of pairs of shoes a woman has is a mutable number. Like the results of an opinion poll, it is valid only for that moment. Shoes are continually added and subtracted from a wardrobe.

Also -- and this is a point of contention between Cricket and me -- it's hard to decide which shoes should be counted. Do I have to count my riding boots, which are really sports equipment rather than shoes? Do I have to count the old tennis shoes I keep on the drier for fluffing up goose down jackets?

What about old shoes, shoes I've had for two or three years and that I'm keeping in case I find a new dress to go with them? If shoes are not in current circulation, do I have to count them?

Do I have to count the 12 pairs of shoes I culled out to give away? Do bedroom slippers count? If they do, do I have to count the ones I never wear but I keep around because the baby likes to play with them? Do I have to count the silk pumps with hand-painted flowers on them that I wore in my first wedding and are too pretty to throw away, even though they've gotten sort of mildewed and I really want to forget that wedding anyway?

Cricket thinks everything should be counted. Under his formula, I have 73 pairs of shoes, about 69 pairs too many.

I think only shoes you currently wear when you dress up to go out should be counted. Under that formula, I have 38 pairs of shoes, a perfectly defensible number.

What men don't understand is that women's wardrobes require

many different shoes. For instance, I have seven pairs of blue shoes, including jellies, bright blue flats, bright blue low heels, light blue high heel sandals, blue dress-up heels with a black patent leather swatch, clunky shoes with a buckle and a medium heel for wearing with pants, and plain blue "sensible" pumps.

Each outfit in a woman's closet requires shoes of a certain color with heels of a certain height, all combined in either a dressy or casual style. And of course you have to have summer and winter shoes.

My friend, Rhett Taylor, permanently solved the problem of shopping for shoes. A captain in the Air Force, she was stationed in Korea at one time. While she was there, she took advantage of the cheap, skilled labor and had 66 pairs of shoes made.

"I just took them a pair of my favorite shoes and had them make me three pairs in every color," she said. In each color, she got one-inch, two-inch and three-inch heels. They are all made of eelskin, her favorite material, and they are all in a simple, but elegant, style.

I thought it was an eminently sensible thing to do, but Cricket was stunned that anybody would buy 66 pairs of shoes all at once.

Before I grew up and realized that the need for many shoes is a fact of gender, I thought my shoe fetish was an inheritance from my mother. My mother truly loves buying shoes, to the point that she will buy shoes for everyone in the family, not just herself.

This would be a welcome gesture except for one thing. The shoes Momma buys never fit. They may be darling shoes, but they don't fit.

As my daddy says, "Flo buys shoes by color, not size."

If she sees a cute pair of shoes on sale and they are within three sizes of her size, she buys them. Then she puts Kleenex in the toes or takes them to the shoe shop to be stretched.

That is fine for her, but she does it to me, too. All my life she has bought me darling shoes that didn't fit. When I look at the size seven box and say, "But Momma, I wear a nine," she says airily, "Oh, I thought you wore a 7 1/2...Well, these look a little big. Just scrunch up your toes."

One Christmas when I came home from college, I found she had bought me a cocktail dress and had a pair of peau de soie shoes dyed to match. The shoes were too small, and by the time the holidays were over,

I was crippled from hobbling around on the cocktail circuit in my color-coordinated outfit.

I personally don't care how cute shoes are, if they don't fit I don't want to wear them. It's hard for me to feel sexy in a pair of shoes when one foot has bleeding blisters and the other has gone numb all the way up to my knee.

I do share Momma's penchant for buying shoes on sale. Between the two of us, we tried mightily to keep the Craddock-Terry shoe company in business. We would have succeeded, too, but we were also trying to keep the Consolidated Shoe Co. Outlet Store in business.

Having been reared in the shadow of shoe factory outlet stores, it kills me to pay more than $20 for a pair of shoes. Imagine my pain last week at having to fork over $28 for a pair of baby size six shoes for 14-month-old Katherine Bolling!

That's it. She's going to have to wear those shoes till she goes to school. She'll just have to scrunch up her toes.

CHAPTER 26

Caught with Our Vents Open

After a week at sub-freezing temperatures, mostly sub-zero temperatures, you'll excuse me if I feel like we have invented winter here.

Don't tell me there are places where winter is like this all the time.

Ken Mittendorf of Manakin tells of the winters he spent in northern Maine, out past where I-95 ends. "When I got there, the snow was piled up higher than a car on each side of the road. I thought they had really high banks there. But it was all snow."

And my grandfather used to tell of his family pioneering in North Dakota. That was B. C., Before Current. Without electric blankets, no human could tolerate the winter there, and they soon moved to tropical Indiana.

I was beginning to feel like a pioneer myself last week, or perhaps a cave dweller. There is hardly anything more primitive than living without running water. If you don't have water, you can't have a cup of coffee, you can't mix up juice, you can't wash dishes, you can't wash clothes, you can't brush your teeth, you can't flush the commode or wash your face and hands.

We really got caught with our vents open. The pipes under our kitchen froze, the pipe to the barn froze and a pipe in the well froze. We were out celebrating the inauguration of Republican Governor George Allen when it happened. The Democrats had predicted, quite accurately as it turned out, that hell would freeze over on that day.

When we got home at, ahem, some wee hour of the morning, we found we had no water. It was around 10 degrees and blowing. So my husband, Cricket, went down in the well to reconnoiter. Froze up.

Cricket basically spent the next two days in the well, except for a few hours he spent driving around in the sleet on icy roads to borrow water and buy pipes and fittings. He wired the well for 220, hooked up a heater and cloaked the affected area with old campaign banners that said "Robin Williams for Delegate."

When the pipe thawed, it burst, spewing several inches of water into the well. That night, during yet another ice storm, Cricket rigged a light in the well and, standing on a cinder block to keep his feet out of the water, replaced the broken pipe.

Meanwhile, I was attempting to perform basic survival chores in the house using the teakettle and assorted containers of water. I spent the week trying to keep cats, dogs, horses and humans fed, watered and dry.

By the time we got water back in the house, the trough at the barn was getting low. Then we got to do my favorite thing: hook five or six hoses together to reach across the property. Normally I do that during the annual summer drought, cursing the kinks in the hoses as I make 25 trips from spigot to bush and back trying to adjust the flow.

This is an even more frustrating task when undertaken at zero degrees across an icy pasture. But there was no choice. The horses refused to drink Gatorade, and the goldfish in the trough were flopping around in about four inches of water.

I assembled our collection of hoses, some neatly coiled in the garage, some hidden under piles of hay, and dragged them into the kitchen to thaw. Then I dragged them outside and began stringing them together. They weren't long enough, so I kept having to search for one more hose. The long one at the barn had one end frozen into the ice in the pasture trough. I tried chipping it out with a hoe, but all I did was hack up the hose.

I finally found a hose with a bent end where one of the horses had stepped on it. Cricket was able to screw it on using pliers and we were in business, sort of. The faucet at the house was frozen, so Cricket thawed it with a torch. By then, one of the hose sections had frozen up again. When we got that resolved, the bent joint leaked so badly that only a trickle of water actually reached the trough.

That was the only time in a week of repairing pipes, hauling water and wiring heaters that Cricket lost his temper. During this ordeal, we also learned about a new weather-related phenomenon, rolling blackouts. This is when you put heaters in the well and under the house to thaw the pipes so you can water your livestock and use the W. C. without filling the tank manually and the power company turns your power off.

The power company regards flushing commodes and running VCRs for housebound children as non-essential uses of electricity. The power company doesn't realize that in the country, where most people have a well, being without power means being without water, too.

Our power went out one night for an hour or so, and for a couple of days we didn't have hot water in the kitchen, but we survived it all. The house was pretty much a wreck, what with hoses all over the kitchen, salt we tracked in, wood chips in a path from the door to the fireplace and horse blankets drying out before the fire.

But we didn't wreck the car, we didn't run out of heating oil (thank you, Marsh Oil Company for making a delivery on New Year's Day) and we didn't have to pay someone zillions of dollars to fix the pipes because one of the adults in this household (not me) knows How To Fix Things.

We sure are lucky.

Do-It-Yourself Funerals
Are More Satisfying

The last time the temperature fell below 95 degrees, I was swept up in a wavelet of energy and trimmed the hedge around our cemetery. One of the carpenters working on the addition, whom I've come to know better than some of my relatives by now, glanced over the hedge one day and noticed the tombstones.

"Is someone buried there?" he asked nervously.

"Oh yes," I answered with a fond smile. "There's Errol Flynn, Jupiter and Rally Bar."

He looked at me for a long moment. Finally he said, "Cats?"

"Flynn was a cat. He's buried under those rocks. The two headstones are for a dog and a pony," I said. "They are buried out in the paddock. The tombstones used to be out there, too, but it was too hard to bush hog around them, so we moved them over next to the cat's grave."

He just stared at the granite headstones, and I began to imagine his dinner-table conversation at home that night. "You know that Williams job I've been telling you about? Well, that woman has horses and dogs buried in her back yard! And got tombstones for them!"

They're nice ones, too. Perk Perkinson made them for me. He's retired now, but he was a highly skilled stonecutter in his day and had a monument business in Church Hill.

Perk might as well have given the stones to me, for all he charged me. Stone monuments are high, too high to bestow lightly on a pet's grave.

Believe me, I didn't erect tombstones for Jupiter the pony and Rally the dog lightly. In my estimation, they were deserving of commemorative works on the order of the Victor Emmanuel Monument in Rome.

It's impossible to explain to someone who has never been attached to an animal just what emotional support pets provide. Santa Claus brought me Jupiter in 1959, and that pony helped me keep the traumas of life in perspective throughout my childhood and teen years.

Rally Bar, likewise, was my best friend and consolation during my unhappy marriage and many subsequent years as a divorcee. That dog, a long-haired, black-and-silver German shepherd who looked more like a wolf, went everywhere I went and knew every word I said.

I've never been able to write about her because I could never express her devotion to me. To try would be to damn her with faint praise.

Jupiter died at age 28 one July. He had been farmed out to various family friends over the years, but when Cricket and I got married, I brought him to live with us.

He was no longer the fire-breathing, immortal steed of my imaginative childhood but a rather meek old man who was content to stare at a gum tree all day. Still, it made me happy to look out the window and see him there.

Anne Hunter Smith, a neighbor's child, rode him some. A month before Jupy died, we dressed him up and Anne rode him in a horse show. I had visions of Anne and Jupiter's sharing a lengthy career together. It never occurred to me he would die and I was devastated when he did.

When a horse dies in July, you can't spend a lot of time making arrangements for disposing of the body. Dead livestock around here normally goes to the Deep Run kennels, but I couldn't do that to Jupy. So, in an unparalleled act of compassion, Cricket, at considerable expense, hired a backhoe to bury Jupiter at home.

Jupy didn't get much of a funeral service, what with the meter running on the backhoe, but we did have a wake. I was surprised that the neighbors didn't come around with cakes and pies, but my daddy drove 30 miles to see me and we spent the evening telling Jupiter stories.

"Remember the time...?"

The next day Anne Hunter Smith came over to see the grave. I was a little concerned about how the five-year-old would take the loss of "her" pony, so as we walked out to the fence, I said gently, "Jupiter has gone to be with Jesus."

Anne was the veteran of several cat funerals, though, and she took it fine. Looking through the fence at the broad expanse of freshly turned earth, she nodded and said, "Jupiter's up in heaven giving little dead children rides."

Momma had little stone markers made for some of her favorite cats when I was little, and I decided my grief would be partially assuaged if I had a marker made for Jupy. So I went to see Perk Perkinson and subjected him to several hours' worth of Jupiter's life story.

He wrote down the pony's name and dates and said he'd fix me up something.

When I went back a couple of weeks later, Perk proudly brought out a giant tombstone on a forklift. He had obviously been deeply moved by my recital of Jupy's adventures, and he had made me a huge, polished granite tombstone with "Jupiter 1955 - 1983" cut in the face.

I had to stop him from putting it in the trunk of my Mustang. The stone must have weighed 300 pounds, and we never would have gotten it out again. So he put a board on the passenger seat and put it in the front seat. It mashed the seat down to the floor but I was too thrilled to care.

Cricket was out of town and there was no one to help me unload the stone. I rode around with it in the front seat for days, worried to death that someone would steal it. Over the phone one night Cricket explained the rather limited appeal of a 300-pound stone with "Jupiter" on it.

When Cricket came home, he drove into the pasture, opened the car door and pushed the stone out. There it lay until November, when we got a stone for Rally to go with it.

On Friday night after Thanksgiving that year, Cricket and I spent several hours in the woods down the road digging a grave for Kate, a black German shepherd who belonged to our friend Stuart Johnson. She had been hit by a car.

Later that same night, Rally went to sleep in the den in her magnificent silver coat. I was a little deranged over her death, and while Cricket went down to Kate's grave to retrieve our shovels, I decided I couldn't put Rally in the ground. I wanted to have her stuffed.

Cricket wisely got me outside to help him dig another giant hole. (You don't realize how large German shepherds are until you go to bury one.) While we were digging, Cricket asked me where I intended to keep a stuffed German shepherd.

It turns out that actually digging the grave and burying your loved one yourself is enormously therapeutic. The physical effort gives you an outlet for your emotions. I still cried when we shoveled the dirt over that handsome, warm body, but I had a sense of completeness, of catharsis when I settled down with my tired muscles.

When my beautiful long-haired yellow cat, Flynn, died last fall, Cricket did all the digging. But I held my friend of 13 years, laid him in his grave and talked about how wonderful he was.

Too bad we can't go back to burying people that way. In fact, there's a lot people could learn from pet funerals.

Kay Higgins says, "When I die, I want Stuart Johnson to conduct the funeral."

Stuart does do good funerals. He has had a lot of practice, burying beloved dogs. He speaks fondly and knowingly about the deceased, which rarely occurs at human funerals anymore.

The Episcopalians are the worst. Their funerals could be for anybody. I've never been to an Episcopal funeral in which the minister seemed to have any personal knowledge of the funeralee. You'd think in that situation a friend of the family would give the eulogy, but nobody ever seems to think of that.

Kay is right. I think I'll get Stuart to do my funeral, too.

CHAPTER 28

Nana's Program for Young Ladies
Who Wish to Get Married

My husband, Cricket, has a whole raft of friends who enjoy teasing him about Katherine Bolling, his baby daughter. Recalling Cricket's frisky days as a bachelor, these friends predict that he will not be so indulgent of boyish behavior and rampant hormones when Katherine Bolling is 16. They have a grand time imagining his reaction when some fellow drives up in a van with a waterbed in the back and honks for his daughter.

Cricket's reply is to say that he has already made a reservation for Katherine Bolling in the convent.

I imagine raising a teenaged daughter has never been easy and these days is probably harder than ever. Girls -- and grown women, too -- think sleeping with a fellow is just part of the dating deal. For some reason, there's no stigma attached to pregnancy or abortion.

I find all that pretty fantastic. When my mother turned 16, in 1940, every girl and her mother knew the way to lose a man was to sleep with him. That was still the conventional wisdom when I turned 16, in 1966.

At least, it was the conventional wisdom in our family.

My grandmother, Flo Crisman Neher, had the best understanding of men probably of any woman in the world. She coached my aunt and my mother through many years of prom-trotting and full dance cards and guided them as they were courted by the men they married.

Nana, as we grandchildren called her, gave me a lot of good advice during my single years, too. Nana's Program for Young Ladies Who Wish to Get Married needs very little adaptation to the modern social scene. Human nature is such that the old rules still work the best, no matter how bizarre they might seem at first glance.

The basic tenet of the program is this: The way to get married is don't act married until you are married. This has more to do with laundry than sex. You can indulge in some hugging and kissing without jeopardizing your chances, but if you want a fellow to propose, don't ever, ever, under any circumstances, do his laundry.

The old saw about the wisdom of purchasing a cow when the milk is readily available holds true today. The key word is "available."

You can't be too available. You have to go along and live your life as though you are going to continue being single. That means you can't start practicing being married in hopes that your fellow will like it and decide to propose. You make him too comfortable and that's where he'll leave the relationship: comfortable.

"Comfortable" means that you look out for the details of his life like clean clothes and home cooked meals. It means that he can count on you to feed his dog and straighten up the house when he's gone. It means that you're on call for socializing or errands, that you're available.

Living determinedly single takes steely self-discipline sometimes, especially when you're going with a fellow who seems like The One. Say your honey-bunch has been out of town for a couple of days. The relationship has gotten to the point where you are spending every second or third evening together. While honey-bunch is away, a fellow at work asks you to go to the movies Friday night.

Since honey-bunch is away, you and he haven't made definite plans for Friday, although you're 99 percent sure you'll end up seeing him that night. What to do?

Nana's answer is to go to the movies with your co-worker. This kills five birds with one stone and will do wonders for your relationship with honey-bunch.

By continuing to see other men up until honey-bunch proposes, you keep him in perspective. You're not so dependent on him for your social life that you forget yourself and do "just one, teensy-weensy load of laundry."

Continuing to see other men reminds you that there are other, attractive men in the world. Besides, having dates is more fun than doing laundry.

Continuing to see other men reminds honey-bunch that there are other, attractive men in the world, therefore he'd better mind his Ps and Qs. Men are basically lazy about their social life. But if you're seeing other men, he's going to have to make an effort, i.e., call ahead, to see you.

Continuing to see other men helps you plan your week instead of sitting around waiting for honey-bunch to call and tell you to drive over. It also spares you the temptation of calling him when you can't wait any longer for him to call you.

Continuing to see other men makes you more attractive in honey-bunch's eyes. He will wonder constantly whom you're seeing and what you're doing. Instead of your being an adjunct to his personal comforts, right up there with a six-pack and Monday Night Football, you will become the center of his thoughts.

The first time you tell honey-bunch you can't see him might be awkward. Don't be defensive or confrontational about it. As Nana always said, "Keep a light touch." She also said, "Don't lie, but don't tell him everything you know."

Say what you really feel: "I'd love to clean out the garage with you Saturday, but I'm afraid I'm tied up that day." It's all right to offer another day. You don't want to humiliate the guy by making him say, Well, how about Tuesday? How about Wednesday? Plus, when you counteroffer -- "Maybe we could get together Sunday instead" -- you're letting him know you really do want to see him.

You'll feel as though you're taking a huge gamble. What if he gets mad and issues an ultimatum or says he doesn't want to see you at all? DON'T cave in and change your plans for him, no matter how mad he gets or how exciting the date sounds. If it's that exciting, he's known about it long enough to call you ahead.

If he's really interested in you, he'll come back, even if he has to sulk a few days. DON'T PHONE HIM. (No texting, either.) If he's not interested in you, this will pique his interest. Remember, that which is unattainable is more desirable.

If he's really not interested in you, you haven't lost anything. (This is easier said than believed. Just remember you don't have to settle for a man on his terms; there are plenty of men you can have on mutual terms.)

The only drawback to Nana's Program for Young Women Who Wish to Get Married is that it takes an awful lot of self-discipline to carry through. You really need a friend, someone who is not emotionally involved with honey-bunch, to back you up on it.

My parents announced their engagement in 1941, during World War II. Shortly before my daddy was sent overseas, he wrote Momma a letter that created great consternation in Momma's household.

There is still a controversy today over what the letter said. Whatever Daddy wrote and whatever he meant, Nana's interpretation was that Daddy was getting cold feet about the wedding. Momma cried, but Nana made her send Daddy's ring back.

As luck would have it, Momma had recently mailed Daddy a package with a new, popular record in it. The ring and the record arrived the same day. In light of the ring and the accompanying letter calling off their engagement, Daddy decided Momma had mailed him the flip side of the record, which was "Jingle Jangle Jingle, Ain't You Glad You're Single?"

Nana didn't want her daughter hanging around waiting for some man who wasn't sure about his feelings. As it turned out, the thought of losing Momma brought Daddy's feelings into sharp focus: they made up through the mail and were married two weeks after Daddy came home from the war. But Nana saw to it that Momma continued to see other men during the two years Daddy was overseas. Daddy laughingly admits: "Flo and I didn't start going steady until the day we got married."

Another one of Nana's dictums was, "Let him do the pursuing." Men like to make the moves, but women today seldom give them a chance. "Girls do not call boys on the telephone."

Hold off on the hugging and kissing. If you are too amorous on the first (second, third, etc.) date, then he will assume you are amorous with these mysterious Other Men. No matter how modern or progressive your honey-bunch is, he wants to believe you reserve your affection for him.

Other Men don't have to be Tom Hanks or Robert Redford. Other Men don't have to be men at all. Other Men can simply be Other Plans, as in, "Oh, sweetheart, I'm so sorry, I've made Other Plans Saturday night. If I'd known sooner you wanted to go out..."

No need to be specific about the nature of your Other Plans. Let him wonder.

Be sure you do have other plans. Don't lie and play games. For your own sake, you should keep your life full.

Denying yourself the short-term gratification of "settling in" has advantages even if the long-term relationship doesn't work out. The main one is that when things fall apart, you've got a life of your own to continue with. If you've spent the last six months waiting by the phone and doing honey-bunch's laundry, you're going to have a big void to fill when you break up.

Also, if the relationship doesn't work out, at least you've maintained your dignity. The double standard still exists and will exist unto eternity. A guy can throw himself at a girl and come out of it looking good even if he doesn't win her, but a girl just looks like the fool she is.

On the other hand, if you follow Nana's advice and honey-bunch does propose, you'll never have to doubt his affection. He wasn't trapped, he pursued you because he wanted you.

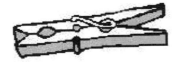

CHAPTER 29

Addiction
Is in the Eye of the Beholder

I n my on-going effort to get my husband, Cricket, to quit smoking, I've tried every conceivable approach short of saying "It's me or the cigarettes." (I had a husband one time who said to me, "It's me or the horse," which prompted me to load up the mare in question and return to Virginia. I probably would have divorced him anyway, nevertheless, the lesson that ultimatums do not work has stuck with me ever since.)

I've nagged. I've begged. I've cried. I've challenged. I've voiced contemptuous criticism, all to no avail.

The only time he quit for any length of time was when we were courting. Once we were married he gradually took up the habit again. It's well-nigh impossible to recreate the circumstances of our courtship, so I'm left looking for another approach.

The approach that would work on me if I were a smoker is the Shared Happiness Tactic. In this approach, you tell your smoking spouse, "It was one thing for you to risk your health and your life when you were single. But now that you have my happiness in your hands, it's not fair of you to continue this unhealthy behavior."

Cricket may be moved by this approach but not enough to quit smoking.

Dear Abby and other authorities on the subject always stress that smoking is an addiction and nagging and recriminations just strain the relationship and reinforce the smoker's determination to smoke. Personally, I think labeling smoking an addiction just gives smokers an easy excuse not to quit.

Most of the time I try to ignore people's cigarettes, but smoking is

131

such a nasty, irritating, stupid habit that I get kind of rabid about it some-times. Whenever I find the baby eating butts out of the ashtray, for in-stance, I get upset.

Cricket doesn't like that, either, but what really upset him was the day we found Katherine Bolling drooling some brown mess and it turned out she was sucking a nugget of Gravy Train. I thought that was funny, myself.

My latest inspiration in the stop-smoking campaign is the Shared Suffering Tactic. In this approach, you tell your smoking spouse, "I will give up something I'm addicted to so we can suffer together and encour-age each other."

The problem with this approach is that I don't have any nasty, irritat-ing, stupid habits to give up, horses and politics aside.

Nevertheless, I broached the subject with Cricket and was elated when he was willing at least to discuss it. He seemed intrigued by the pos-sibility of dictating some limits on my behavior. That made me nervous.

My idea was to give up something like coffee. I love my one cup of coffee in the morning to the point that I will drink it even when I don't have time to enjoy it. And I will fix a second cup if I didn't get to savor the first one. This is classic behavior for an addict: The first hit is always the best, yet the addict continues to do more in the vain hope that successive hits will come close to the pleasure of the first one.

Drinking coffee isn't as dangerous as smoking, but it still seemed like a parallel sacrifice for me to make. As alternatives, I thought I could give up wearing colored stockings, being a night owl or going out to do errands 15 minutes before Cricket comes home from work, all of which annoy him.

Cricket wanted to know if I was serious about the Shared Suffering Tactic. Sensing victory I said yes, yes. So then he announced his terms: "I'll give up smoking if you give up the telephone."

The telephone?

How would I arrange babysitters, make lunch dates and doctor's ap-pointments, boss around my surrogate daughter, Marilynn Ware, arrange babysitters, engage a paperhanger, organize Republican volunteers, hire a yardman, arrange babysitters, find homes for abandoned animals and keep track of my peripatetic parents?

Actually, I don't enjoy making any of those phone calls, with the exception of bossing Marilynn around -- and to tell the truth, that's gotten to be a thankless job lately. But it does seem to be the business of my life to get those things done and using the telephone is a lot more efficient than writing letters or driving around.

Unfortunately, a lot of the people I have to get a hold of are only available in the evening when Cricket is at home waiting for dinner or waiting for me to sit down for a chat. So I do understand his irritation at my telephone time.

I'm irritated by it, too. I hate having to make telephone calls and I'm further irritated by anything that impedes the progress of my phoning, such as people who are not home when I call or clerks who put me on hold for more than 3 seconds.

This new service, "call waiting," is of particular irritation to me. I cannot for the life of me understand why anyone except a doctor, fireman or rescue squad worker needs this service. Why would an ordinary person at home need to know if someone else was trying to call him while he was talking on the phone?

When I worked at the Times-Dispatch, the office phones had call waiting and it was very distracting to me and obviously irritating to the person I was interviewing at the time. My desk mate, who is still there, had hers disconnected.

My friends who have call waiting are polite about checking the other caller and returning to me immediately, but I still find it insulting to have my call interrupted. If the other call is that important, the caller will call back.

On the other hand, answering machines don't bother me. Although I would prefer to reach the person directly and conclude my business in one call, I like the efficiency of leaving a message and accomplishing something in a short call. Also, if it weren't for answering machines, I would have no contact with my family at all.

So when Cricket asked me to give up making phone calls, I was dubious about carrying on the business of my life. If I were to rely on incoming phone calls, my telephone conversations would be limited to listening to taped pitches for vacuum cleaners, answering surveys about which fast food restaurants I patronize ("None"), and refusing great bargains on cemetery plots and light bulbs sold by handicapped salesmen.

Then I remembered Pam Ottley.

Pam Ottley is living proof that you can conduct a business without making phone calls. Pam has never dialed an outgoing phone call in her life. Her friends and clients know this, so they call her. The result is that Pam spends every single moment she is at home on the telephone. Now there is a person whose husband could, justifiably, disconnect the telephone.

But I don't think Billy Ottley smokes.

CHAPTER 30

The Magic Carpet Pony

When Santa Claus delivered Jupiter in 1959, he brought a magic carpet with powers the jolly old elf himself scarcely understood. I was nine that Christmas and I'd ridden horses as long as I could remember, but that brilliant bay pony changed the meaning of "riding" for me. You didn't ride Jupiter; he carried you away. The moment you slid across his back, Jupiter transported you to exotic places and romantic times. He carried me safely through four wars and over thousands of fences -- and past the innumerable traumas of growing up.

On Jupiter's back I rode through the Pee Dee Swamp to warn Francis Marion, the Swamp Fox of the Revolution, of a British attack. On Jupiter's back I fought Indians and found the Cumberland Gap.

Still another day, we were ambushed by Yankees and Jupy raced back to Jeb Stuart's camp with me clinging to the saddle in wounded glory. Together we rewrote history, galloping across Texas to get reinforcements for Travis and Bowie at the Alamo.

When it came to go-for-the-gold, never-say-die and thrill-of-a-lifetime, the Black Stallion wasn't a patch on Jupiter.

With the fearlessness of childhood, I rode my father's horses almost as soon as I could walk. When I was six, I rode a horse named Sox at a local show, flawlessly putting the big horse through his gaits. Unfortunately, Sox's gaits were not precisely what the judges called for. Nevertheless, I came breathlessly out of the ring saying, "I almost won, Daddy, I almost won!" My parents were mystified. "How do you figure that?"

"Well, they called number 62, and my number was 63."

Daddy went pony hunting the next day. My first pony was a big, spoiled mare named Twinkle, about whom the less said, the better. I was, as horse people say, grossly overmounted. The last straw in our disastrous career together came the day Twinkle jumped out of the ring with me at a horse show. Someone grabbed her bridle as she bolted past and Daddy snatched me off her back. "Don't you ever get on that pony again," he ordered.

So Daddy went pony hunting again, determined to do better this time. One afternoon he and my grandfather went to Mountain Glen Farm near Orange, Va. Daddy had $300 in his pocket, just in case he found the right animal.

While he was there, he saw a flashy blood bay pony standing on the concrete slab in front of the barn. A man was grooming the pony, who stood perfectly still, proudly accepting the attention as though he knew his burnished coat shined like a new penny and his jet black mane set off his muscular neck. He was a registered Welsh pony, 13 hands (52 inches) of spit and polish and spit in your eye.

Daddy didn't even price him. He just thought, *Wouldn't it be fabulous to own a pony like that?*

Daddy called at the farm again and this time he had an agent with him. They looked at the handsome bay four-year-old pony and Daddy knew he couldn't settle for anything else.

"Buy him," he told the agent.

He paid $800 for Jupiter. It was an exorbitant sum for a pony in those days, especially for a pony that would never be resold.

Don Floyd, a friend of Daddy's, picked the pony up and kept him at his place for a couple of weeks. About noon on Christmas Eve, it began to sleet and the phone rang. It was Don. "If you want me to bring this pony, I've got to come now."

Daddy said come on, and Momma whisked me off to the grocery store. That night in our cosy stable, they groomed him and tied a red ribbon on his halter.

The next morning, we three children came downstairs and excitedly fell upon our gifts from Santa Claus. Momma and Daddy had left a note in my stocking, which I failed to find for some time. The suspense must have been unbearable, because after awhile Momma said, "Robin, don't you think you'd better check your stocking again?"

There was the note, printed awkwardly with horseshoes for some of the letters. "Dear Robin, I am waiting for you down at the barn. Please come soon. Jupiter."

I'm sure my ecstasy was worth $800.

As Jupiter and I rode out across the field in front of our stable, it was as if I'd been given a magic carpet. From then on, Jupiter took me anywhere I wanted to go, from the winner's circle to the ends of my imagination.

Of course, he did it on his terms. Jupiter was too independent to be anybody's lackey. He dutifully carried me over hill and dale and post-and-rail, but only after I'd spent an hour trying to catch him. He'd wait until I could almost lay my hand on his halter, then he'd gallop to the farthest corner of the pasture. I devised elaborate schemes that involved toting prodigious amounts of feed and catching all the other horses, but I couldn't catch him if he didn't want to be caught.

He was the cock of the walk at our barn. Daddy loved to trade horses and we had a lot of turnover. Every time a new horse came into the field, Jupiter went over and introduced himself by kicking him two or three times. Daddy used to say Jupiter could trot backwards in his eagerness to kick other horses.

He also liked to kick dogs. We had a border collie named Pete who never learned. He loved to herd the horses back to the barn when we called them. Jupiter didn't cotton to being herded, and he could kick so fast Pete didn't know what hit him. Jupy wouldn't even raise his head from grazing, just zing a hind foot out and snap it back.

Jupiter could live on air, too. He stayed fat, no matter how much I rode him. Daddy was always telling my brother Cris, who had feed duty, to "cut Jupiter's feed down." In exasperation one day, Cris said, "I've got him down to one oat."

You couldn't be around Jupiter without sensing that he was alive. He always wanted to run as hard as he could and jump as high as he could. Daddy saw him jump out over a four-foot high paddock fence in the snow one time, make a circle and jump back in. His exuberance could be excessive at times, but you had to love him for it.

Jupiter was always running away with me when we were foxhunting.

I still have the pelham bit I hunted him in, and the shanks are bent from my pulling on them. When I went flying past Daddy, out of control again, he'd shout, "Just don't pass the hounds!"

On one of my first hunts, when I was about 10, Jupiter disdained a creek crossing and went down the sheer bank. As he scrambled up the other side, I fell off, tearing my brand new corduroy jodhpurs as Jupiter galloped off after the other horses.

I was mortified. Jupiter was totally unremorseful. If you're not good enough to stay with me, that's your problem, he seemed to say.

But Jupiter didn't embarrass me much. More often, he saved my skin when I made outrageous boasts on his behalf. I rode that little pony over a lot of fences I'd hesitate to jump with a horse today. Jupiter had the right stuff -- and he knew it, too, the cocky son-of-a-gun.

Daddy often took me with him when he foxhunted with other clubs, but there was always the embarrassing possibility that Jupy would run away. On one occasion when we particularly wanted to appear civilized, Daddy decided to tranquilize Jupiter to slow him down. He gave the pony a shot before we left home, and then, just outside town, he pulled over and gave him a booster.

It didn't faze Jupiter a bit. He dragged me all over central Virginia just as fast as ever.

Jupiter wasn't above asserting his independence in the show ring, either. Every so often, he would refuse a fence just to remind me that I rode -- and won -- at his sufferance. Most of the time, though, he suffered me to win. The walls of my bedroom were covered with the ribbons he won. Jupiter provided me with a truckload of silver bon-bon dishes and a trousseau of trays, plates and goblets.

Once, he won the magnificent sum of $7. I had visions of his becoming a source of income as well as pleasure until Daddy presented me with a bill for entry fees.

Jupiter was a ham and he loved going to horse shows, as a spectator as well as a performer. Once when I was in the ring on another horse, Jupiter untied himself from the trailer and walked over to the ring to watch. He found Momma and Daddy and stood with them, turning his head to follow the action.

After I moved on to horses, Jupiter carried my younger brother, Cris, to victory. There had been talk earlier of selling him when I outgrew him. After all, ponies are expensive pets, and they live forever. Well, almost forever. But Jupiter had won our hearts and he had a home for life.

My childhood friendship with Jupiter deepened in high school. Although we had other horses that needed exercise and training, some afternoons I took off cross-country on Jupiter. There in the foothills of the Blue Ridge Mountains on a slightly untamed pony, I dealt with the disappointments of teenage life. So what if I didn't get chosen to be a cheerleader? Being a cheerleader would have conflicted with my serious interest in showing horses. So what if the wrong fellow asked me to the dance? I didn't have time to agonize over adolescent crushes with a barn full of horses to ride. And surely exploring the woods with a trusty companion, counting the hawks and buzzards, chasing the deer was more fun than hanging around the drugstore hoping some pimply-faced boy would say hi.

Soon I was off at college with no time for ponies, no matter how cute or cocky. When I got married, though, we began to talk of the day when my little girl would have Jupiter to ride. It was reason enough to get pregnant as soon as possible. Jupy was then 15. But I never had that daughter. In my efforts to be a good wife, I found myself living on someone else's terms. I was being penned up in smaller and smaller corrals until one day in desperation I fled.

I went home, naturally, and my parents were very supportive. But divorce was still somewhat scandalous in those days and I wrestled with guilt and feelings of failure. I spent a lot of time sitting on the fence watching the horses in the pasture and reminiscing about my adventures with Jupiter. He was well into middle age and had mellowed a bit, but I suspected he could still save the Alamo or carry me away from childhood disappointments.

I decided to give it a try. One mild afternoon early in December, I put a saddle on Jupiter and went for a long ride. He didn't look much like the magic carpet steed of my childhood. He had a shaggy brown winter coat and "leg warmers" that completely covered his hooves. But the moment I got on him and felt that familiar step, those movements that were an extension of my own body, I was flooded with a feeling of security, of being home. We both enjoyed being out in the open, cantering across a big field with no fences in sight. Let's go to Egypt! Jupiter seemed to say.

As I began making a life of my own, I found that Jupiter was more to me than a solace in troubled times. Reminiscing about our youthful adventures, I began to see in Jupy a role model for getting the most out of life.

Jupiter never asked how high the fences were or whom he had to beat. He just jumped. After he had demolished the competition in his own division, he cheerfully outjumped horses a foot taller than he. Once I even had the nerve -- or the faith -- to enter him in a barrel race, a timed event for quarter horses. We rode into the ring, a chubby-cheeked girl with pigtails on a fat pony with an English saddle. The cowhide cowboys on their Western horses snickered. When it was our turn, Jupiter flew around the course, his little legs a blur as he circled the barrels without even slowing down. He won, beating the state champion barrel racer in the process. It was no more than I expected of him, but those cowboys were flabbergasted.

His attitude rubbed off on me and helped me get my first job -- and all the ones thereafter. There wasn't even an opening at the local magazine when I called for an interview. I must have been an unlikely candidate -- a college dropout with no experience. Feeling like an English pony up against Western horses, I went to see the editor. But, Jupy-like, I knew I could do the job. The self-confidence must have worked, because the editor hired me.

While I was roaming around after my divorce, my parents sold the place and moved in town. They found a home for Jupiter and a succession of other little girls showed him.

None was as successful as I, which secretly pleased me. He and I were a team.

When he was 21 and in need of a new pasture, we offered Jupy to a woman who had known him in his prime and had a special fondness for him. Jupy was the perfect baby sitter for her small children. One day on a family ride, her four-year-old fell off and rolled under Jupy's feet. The old pony stopped and patiently held one foot in the air until the child was rescued.

Passed their place once in awhile, I would stop and have a chat. He was fat, gray and happy. My life was in turmoil throughout most of the 1970s, and I longed to have Jupiter with me as a token of stability, a reminder of the magic carpet days when no fantasy was beyond our range.

My second marriage gave me a second chance at a lot of things, among them, my happy childhood. My husband sensed how important Jupiter was to me, and he encouraged me to bring the old pony home at last. I wrote Jupiter's current guardian to invite her to the wedding and tell her that I wanted Jupy back. She wrote back that of course he was mine and I could have him, but she hated to give him up, the children loved him and he was so good with them, and so on.

I didn't feel the first pang of guilt. After all, he was my pony and no one had ever loved him as I did. He was 25 years old and it was time for him to retire where I could look at him every day and remember that there was no dream that couldn't come true.

In high spirits, I went to pick him up. When I found him, I was appalled at the toll the years had taken: He was thin, one ear was crumpled over and he had something wrong with one eye. Furthermore, although it was September, he had the long coat of at least one winter, if not two. He always looked like a teddy bear in the winter, and it took a lot of rubbing to shed all that hair every spring. Obviously, no one had rubbed him that spring.

I cried all the way home. When I unloaded him, I really was afraid he'd keel over and die before I could get him in the barn. I began shoving grain at him and called the vet.

Two days of grain-feeding later, Jupy had perked up considerably.

The vet came, and both of us with a twitch couldn't hold the pony to worm him. He kicked the stall door open and dragged us out into the paddock. Later he slipped out the gate and ran away. And he kicked two dogs.

I was delighted. A week after he came home, I couldn't stand it any longer. I got on him. He walked around a bit and then we trotted. Then he broke into a little canter and, to my astonishment, put his head down and tried to run away. Oh, you spunky pony!

My husband, Cricket, quickly became enamored of the pony, and together we nursed him. For six weeks, we had to inject his eyelid twice a day, a procedure Jupiter stoically accepted. He ended up with partial sight on that side. The crumpled ear was a benign tumor and we couldn't do anything about that. He had other lumps on his body, too.

I was beside myself with excitement at having Jupy back. I was sure that if I could just get him fat again and groom him up, the gray would turn to bay and he -- and I -- would both be youngsters again. In the spring, I rubbed him till he shone. His whiskers and the long hair on his ankles were trimmed. Under a vigorous feeding program, he put on some weight. For three years, I enjoyed sitting on the porch and seeing my old pony in the pasture, knowing he was loved and well cared-for. Cricket and I used to laugh at the way he adopted a particular tree, standing before it and staring at it as if it might move.

Momma resurrected the little saddle I had used. Since I still didn't have a daughter, I co-opted our little neighbor, Anne Smith, to carry out the dream. One Saturday, with Jupiter trimmed and braided and Anne turned out in tiny boots and jacket, we went to a horse show. Jupiter was 28 and Anne was five.

Ponies, I've always heard, are like Oliver Wendall Holmes' Wonderful One-Hoss Shay that lasted 100 years to the day. Nothing goes wrong, they just get worn out and up and die one day.

The horse show was Jupy's swan song. A month later he colicked and died. Colic is very serious in horses, even if the cause of the stomach ache is not. A horse with colic will roll until he ruptures something and dies.

An hour after I found Jupy rolling in pain, the vet was there giving him laxatives and painkillers. I stayed up all night, leading him around, sitting by him while he lay down and rested, whipping him to get up when he tried to roll. By morning, he was doing well enough for me to leave him tied up for an hour or two at a time.

I rode my mare and Jupiter whinnied, as he always did, when we returned. I left him loose in the paddock and went up to the house. When the vet came to check on him two hours later, we walked cheerfully down to the barn.

There is no mistaking death, even from a distance.

"Oh, there he is," I said, my voice dropping off as I realized the vet's visit was unnecessary. Jupy had walked out of the barn and picked a grassy spot under a tulip poplar beside a row of daylilies. There's a bluebird box there, too, where two nestings of bluebirds are raised each summer. In this pleasant spot, he lay down and died.

The rest of the day was spent much as anyone spends making funeral arrangements for a loved one. I called my husband in tears, and he began to look for a backhoe. Daddy called and we cried together. "Remember the time...?" Momma called and we cried together.

In between calls, I combed his mane and tail, braiding his forelock and a lock of his tail to cut off and keep. I patted his still warm body, but it felt strange. He looked stuffed.

They're so dead when they're dead.

When the backhoe came, Cricket made me go inside. By the time I came back out, he had laid a slab of slate at the pony's head, spread grass seed and turned on the sprinkler.

Daddy came over for the wake, and we told Jupiter stories. I kept waiting for all the neighbors to come calling and bringing pies and hams.

I got out some old pictures of Jupiter, but the best pictures of him were in our minds. Daddy shook his head and laughed occasionally at some memory. And we all got choked up. I'd never seen my daddy cry before. In fact, I wondered a bit at his sentimentality, driving 30 miles on a weeknight just to talk about an old pony.

"I'll always picture him jumping the paddock fence in the snow," Daddy said. "You know, that pony had more heart than any horse I've ever seen. He had to, because he didn't have enough leg to jump half the things I saw him go over."

"Is that why you never sold him?" I asked.

Daddy shrugged sheepishly.

I reminded him of what he had always said about owning horses: "They're too expensive to keep as pets. You should never have a horse that isn't for sale."

"Oh, I put a price on Jupiter," he said. "But fortunately no one took me up on it."

That was the first I'd heard of that. "What were you asking for him?"

Daddy smiled, his eyes shining again. "I figured one day that watching you and that biggety little pony take on all comers was worth about a million dollars. Maybe $900,000. I didn't want to be unreasonable."

CHAPTER 31

Boat People and Their Boat Stuff

Having been raised in the mountains with horses, I never think of my family as boat people, but I've noticed recently that everyone in the family, except me, is involved with boats. My parents have comfortable motor cruiser. My younger brother, Cris, has a small power boat. And my older brother, Bo, is a tugboat captain.

My husband, Cricket, would be quick to point out, with only a trace of bitterness, that although he is not involved with boats at the present time, it is a mere technicality. He is still a boat person.

I've never really gotten the boating bug myself, although I keep getting involved with men who are into boats. My first husband's family had a big power boat, the kind with a name like Do-Re-Me composed of the first letters of everybody in the family's name. I remember spending several afternoons in the water near that boat as my ex and his family made good-natured attempts to drown me, under the guise of teaching me to ski.

"One more time, now. You've nearly got it. Next time let go of the tow rope when you fall."

After we went our separate ways, I had some dates with a man who was really into boating. He was a naval officer with command of a destroyer, which, to the chagrin of his crew, he once let me drive. In spite of that breach of national security, he later became an admiral.

Next, I spent some time with a fellow whose family had a 35-foot sailboat, and we cruised around the Chesapeake Bay in it a couple of summers. Then one windy day, one of the spreaders slipped and the mast broke.

It was a pretty wild situation, because, although it was a bright, sunny day and there were other sailboats around us, the high wind made us feel as though we were alone in a storm of legendary proportions.

For one thing, lots of important boat stuff was hanging over the sides in the water or floating freely. The folded mainsail acted like a windsock and kept jerking the boat over sideways. Without propulsion, there was no way to control the direction of the boat. Nevertheless, my date handed me the wheel and told me to "keep it in the wind" while he managed the crisis.

There was another couple on board who knew even less about sailing than I did, but they tried to help by retrieving things with a crab net. In the way of all skippers with inexperienced crews in a crisis, my date shouted impossible orders while heroically hauling in sheets with his teeth and fending off the boom with his foot.

We made it back home under power but the mast was a total loss. They had to replace it with an aluminum one, and my date was never the same again.

Cricket had a boat when we met, a 21-foot Grady White with the suitable name of "High Roller." It was a sporty little number with which he wooed women who weren't prone to motion-sickness. Luckily for me, we had a short, winter courtship that culminated in a pre-boating-season wedding.

During his bachelor years, Cricket and his friends had many wonderful adventures with High Roller, most of which seemed to involve malfunctions of the steering mechanism during a storm 50 miles out at sea.

Cricket also speaks nostalgically of the time several couples spent a boating weekend camped on a sand bar without shade or sunscreen. Then there was the memorable winter night when High Roller broke down, leaving Cricket and Stuart Johnson arguing over which one of them would get to sleep with the only article of warmth on the boat, a German shepherd.

The first summer we were married, we rented a cottage in Urbanna and spent every weekend at the river. The idea was to spend every weekend on High Roller, too. That idea lasted one day. The first time Cricket took me out on his beloved boat, we headed to the middle of the Chesapeake Bay to fish.

Cricket buzzed out to the Bay so fast the hull of the boat rattled against the incoming waves, beating my body to a pulp. He cut the engine at some unmarked spot in the water and announced we were at Cut Channel. While I hung over the side and chummed for bluefish with my breakfast and all the meals I'd eaten in the past week, Cricket baited the hooks.

Almost immediately, he decided the engine didn't sound right, and rather than be stranded in the Bay, he headed back to Urbanna. When we got back to the dock, High Roller and I were both beyond repair.

That was the only time I was ever on High Roller -- when it was in the water, at least. I did clamber over the boat several times during the seven years that it was moored in our garage awaiting engine repairs. Every fall, Cricket would say, "I think my winter project will be rebuilding that engine."

He actually went so far as to take the engine off the boat and break it down into 10,000 pieces, which were carefully piled in boxes and on work benches throughout the basement, the garage and the tool shed. But Cricket prefers doing chores that require the use of a saw, and so the engine parts gathered dust.

It was rather pathetic to see the once-jaunty boat resting on railroad ties many miles from the Bay. What really depressed Cricket was that the cats adopted the bow of the boat as their sundeck. I kept a bowl of cat food up there and almost any time you could see a couple of cats lounging next to the cleats or draped over the coiled bow lines.

After four or five years of this, I broached the subject of selling the boat. Cricket clearly thought this was heretical. Nevertheless, he grudgingly accepted my observation that having a dead boat in the garage for five years was not adding to the value of the property. One day he said in a martyr's voice, "You can sell the boat. I can't do it, but you go ahead."

So I put an ad in the Trading Post and folks began to call. Two men came out to see the boat and Cricket gave them the sales pitch. I watched eagerly through the kitchen window as he described the fabulous vessel that lay underneath six years' accumulation of cat hair and red clay.

When they left and Cricket came inside, I asked, "Well?"

Cricket shook his head sadly. "They wanted it but I wouldn't let them have it. I can't sell my boat. I love my boat."

A year or so later, though, when Cricket was taken with the idea of buying a tractor, he sold the boat. He really sold it this time, and the people actually came and took it out of the garage.

He sold all the engine parts with it, and it was truly astonishing how much room we had in the basement and the garage and the tool shed after Cricket collected all the engine parts and put them in the buyer's truck.

As Cricket helped the man load everything in his truck, he explained what each item was, just so the man would realize what a steal he was getting. "Now this is a brand new Teflon-coated propeller worth $400. And this is..."

He bought a tractor, which he is fond of but which will probably never accord him the same excitement as the boat. As a consolation, I bought him an engraved sign for the tractor that says "High Roller."

CHAPTER 32

Wasting Away in Garbageville

I was wrestling with the wrapping on a new baby gate the other day and as I fell to the floor in exhaustion, abandoning the triumphant gate to its translucent cocoon, my mouth foamed and formed these heretical words: I hate plastic.

Truly, plastic is the curse of our generation. The characteristics that made it popular are, in excess, the same that make it an environmental nightmare. Plastic is the kudzu of manufacturing.

In the 1930s, the federal government promoted the planting of kudzu along thousands of miles of roadway. A hardy, rapid-growing vine, kudzu was hailed as a natural solution to erosion.

Kudzu, of course, turned out to be hardier and faster-growing than anyone in his wildest dreams ever imagined, and thousands of miles of American roadway are bordered by trees and banks on which a solid, endless canopy of kudzu appears to have been draped.

Plastic's primary attraction was that it was an inexpensive, relatively durable substitute for other materials such as glass and paper. The use of plastic packaging was the first big step in the creation of the throwaway society.

Not every throwaway item is plastic, but the use of plastics fostered the throwaway mentality.

Now thousands of miles of American roadway are bordered by trees and banks on which a solid, endless blanket of trash has been thrown.

Throwing away, whether it's plastics or glass or paper or washing machines or tires, is a problem of such rapid growth and sweeping reach that it makes kudzu look like an endangered species.

The growth industry of the 21st century is going to be trash disposal. The population- and garbage-choked Northeastern states are closing landfills right and left. Beaches in those states are being closed too, because garbage is being dumped in the ocean and washing ashore.

Remember the garbage barge from Islip, N.Y., which was rejected by six states and three countries during a four-month odyssey one summer? Don't kid yourself. It could happen in Virginia.

Government officials, bless their souls, are beginning to recognize the magnitude of the problem, but the American people still think the answer to waste disposal is to throw it out the car window.

If you want to see firsthand how bad the trash situation is in this country and how shortsighted public attitude is toward waste disposal, just take a bag and walk around your neighborhood. The volume of trash alongside our roads is simply unbelievable.

A contingent of inmates from James River Correctional Center has been clearing off the State Farm's overgrown fence line on Lee Road lately. Armed with weed-whackers and bush axes, they have peeled back the layer of wildflowers, weeds and seedlings that hid a hillside of animal burrows and human garbage.

It's discouraging to see the array of trash under the weeds because I thought I had that part of the road picked up. I go out walking with the baby in her stroller and pick up the beer cans and drink bottles and cake wrappers along the shoulder. Even when I police the road regularly, I can fill up the storage basket under the stroller before we reach the neighbor's property line.

Last year I cleaned the road thoroughly in late winter then left it untouched for three months. Then, in two days of steady work, I collected three garbage bags lipping full. There were 55 pounds of drink containers, cigarette packs and junk food wrappers along a half-mile stretch of dead end, residential road.

My husband, Cricket, took all that trash to the dump for me, but the county landfill isn't a bottomless pit. As the Free Press reported last week, the life of our landfill is only four to five years under current usage.

What are we going to do with all this trash? In Suffolk, an environmental group is trying to kill an efficient waste-to-steam incinerator project because of environmental and economic concerns. The environmental group proposes recycling as an alternative.

But recycling will only account for about 10 percent of the volume of waste, whereas incineration will dispose of about 95. In addition, by burning its garbage, a municipality can produce steam power for its own use or for sale to private industry.

The truth is that recycling and incineration are not alternatives to each other. The solution to waste disposal is an aggressive pursuit of recycling and incineration...and source reduction and manufacturing reforms.

Source reduction means don't make the stuff in the first place. I venture to guess that source reduction will be the hardest aspect of waste disposal for Americans to handle. If the low cost of plastics and paper is attractive, the throwaway characteristic is indispensable.

In the end, though, throwing away items is going to cost more than using reusable items.

One way or the other, you and I are going to pay for trash disposal. We're going to pay for landfills and incinerator plants and tax incentives to manufacturers to find substitute materials.

We're going to pay taxes so the state can spend $3,000,000 picking up litter. We're going to pay higher costs for products that have been redesigned to be recyclable. And we're going to give up some of the convenience of producing prodigious amounts of trash.

Source reduction is an important, painless-sounding aspect of waste management. What it means is living without certain conveniences that we've grown accustomed to in the throwaway society. Some of that is going to be tough. I know it's a phase I'm going through, but I would find it difficult to do without disposable diapers.

And I like the plastic lenses in my glasses, even though they are so scratched they look like someone roller-skated over them. Plastic, rather than metal, paper clips are nice when working around computer disks.

I'm a long-time advocate of fountain pens, the kind with a bladder you refill from a bottle of ink, but I've recently found a disposable pen that writes just like my fountain pen and doesn't leak, so I've been corrupted there, too.

And I have my share of plastic cameras, hair dryers and tape players that have a limited useable life and unlimited effect on the county landfill.

I could live quite happily for many years, though, if publishers would quit sending me magazines in clear plastic sleeves that I can't remove without tearing up the magazine. It wouldn't bother me a bit to go back to paying deposits on reusable drink bottles, either. If "trash" has value, it doesn't end up on the side of the road.

It might be nice to go back to having things that last. My mother still has the wooden playpen she raised all of us in. It's no thing of beauty and OSHA would probably burn us at the stake for using it, but it has lasted 35 years and saved Momma the expense of buying another one for visiting grandchildren.

And, of course, I'd love to buy a baby gate I could unwrap without a blowtorch.

CHAPTER 33

Foxhunting in February: Rugged, Sensual

There's hardly a hunting morning these days that I don't wake up in the cold made colder by the darkness and think of the old Irishman on his deathbed. The dying foxhunter was asked by his priest if he had any regrets in life and he said, "Yes, I regret that I didn't hunt more before Christmas."

Foxhunting in January and February is a rugged pastime, and its devotees are far outnumbered by those who nod in agreement with the old Irishman. In September and October, during cubbing season — sort of a scrimmage season for young foxhounds and cub foxes -- the footing is good and the pre-dawn meets are a relief after months of summer heat. In November and December, when the serious hunting gets under way, foxhunters enjoy two months of hunting under ideal conditions: the pack has jelled, the footing is still good and the weather is bracing without being a trial of human endurance.

Hunting after the holidays is another experience altogether. The footing is poor at best, treacherous at worst, bringing the constant fear of your horse slipping or falling and throwing both of you to the ground. Creeks become quagmires and jumps are formidable obstacles surrounded by sheets of ice. The temperature is forever in the teens or twenties and compounded by a biting wind.

Ah, but the hounds are lean and muscular and well-seasoned, and the cub foxes have learned the wily tricks of their elders, and the horses are fit enough to keep up with hounds that are keen enough to run a fox all afternoon.

On a sharp winter day, there's no fire as warm as a blaze of speed from an honest hunting horse.

Perhaps my pleasure in dead-of-winter hunting has a nostalgic base. I grew up hunting with my daddy in whatever weather Saturday had to offer. I'm sure there were some pleasant days, but all I remember is coming home in the dark, week after week, with fingers and toes numb and the skin on my face blistered by the cold wind.

Our hearts were high, though, from the exhilaration of the hunt, and we unwound by settling our horses in the cozy stable for the night. Then at last we settled ourselves in the kitchen to eat Momma's chili and tell her about the day. I'm sure there were some nights when we had fried chicken, but all I remember is coming home to Momma's chili.

Daddy and I were still excited and we took turns giving Momma the blow-by-blow: where the hounds ran and how the horses behaved and what happened to the other riders who had balky or hot horses. Momma even acted as though she was really interested. Every now and then, Daddy would interrupt me to say, "Skip the descriptive paragraphs. Just tell what happened."

After dinner I'd take a long hot shower and sleep the sleep of the just.

Foxhunting is such a sensual experience, or rather, a collection of sensual experiences.

When I first get on my horse at the meet I jockey around in my irons, looking for that groove in the saddle that makes me feel attached to the horse. It's no use. It'll take that jog to the first covert to find the groove.

I speak to the master, who, if the temperature is below freezing, asks, "Going swimming today?"

It's his favorite gibe. Once, on a 20-degree day, I took a spill in rain-swollen Beaverdam Creek.

Then I speak to the other riders and the huntsman -- the man who actually directs the hounds. At last -- my favorite part -- I speak to the hounds, noting that Limerick and Treacle and Lyric are out today. Dimple is not. She's close to whelping, too fat to keep up. I count 15 couple, 30 hounds to keep track of today.

I'm a whipper-in, one of the huntsman's helpers, and he tells me he's going to draw along the lake to the dam, then turn and come back by the old dump. He sends me ahead to watch for the fox and keep the hounds in line. I gallop off to my post, finding the groove at last and marveling again at the smooth, ground-eating stride of my horse.

I take up my position on a hillside where I have a view of two fields and part of the lake's shoreline. It's 23 degrees and the wind is noticeable but not too strong to make scenting hopeless. It's strong enough to make me shiver, though, and I listen hopefully for the hounds' voices. If they find a fox quickly, we'll have a run and warm up.

All I hear, though, is the huntsman's voice, urging the hounds to "push him up." Occasionally, he gives the hounds a short command on the horn. As they get closer, I move to the next hilltop. I'm careful to keep the shoreline of the lake in view. One embarrassing day, I missed seeing a fox because he skirted around me hugging the waterline.

There! The hounds speak! But almost immediately the huntsman blows a sour note on his horn, signifying that the hounds are on deer.

I dash off to intercept them, cracking my whip and shouting "'Ware deer! Back to him!" The hounds know they are wrong and as they turn to go back to the huntsman, I note which ones were leading the sinful chase.

The huntsman continues his draw and I continue to move ahead of him, wishing my elegantly slim boots were inelegantly big enough to accommodate thermal socks.

After an hour of walking around vainly searching for a fox, the huntsman confers with the master about where to look next. "Charlie's in his den, laughing at us fools out here on a day like this," he says with a laugh. Several members of the field have decided to quit being foolish and go in. The hard core follows the master and the huntsman across the dam at the foot of the lake.

Before I can move ahead to my new post, the hounds strike. This time they're right, and a pack of parti-colored hounds flies away through the woods beside the lake. The huntsman is galloping with them, blowing "Gone Away" to encourage every hound to join the chase.

Thinking the fox might turn right-handed, I take a different trail. At the top of the ridge, I stop to listen and hear nothing. Either the hounds have run straight out of earshot or they've lost the line. My horse turns his head, ears pricked. Is that the hounds? No, a flock of Canada geese has fooled me again.

I hold my position, listening to the squirrels romping in the dead leaves, watching a great blue heron leave the lake. Soon I must take a chance and move on or risk being left hopelessly behind. Then I hear a soft trit-trot through the leaves. My horse and I stop breathing and watch as a fox trots out onto the trail.

The fox feels our presence and stops to exchange stares. It is a small fox, probably a vixen or a cub, weighing less than 10 pounds. I've never seen this fox before. It is dark red with lots of white on its throat and legs and a well-defined black mask. As it whirls and runs through the woods, I see the white tip of its tail.

When the fox is beyond me, I raise my voice in a view-holloa, a sort of rebel yell: whooooo-ee, whooooo-ee! The huntsman harks the hounds to my voice, and in a moment the hounds are running and singing through the woods again.

Noting that Nimrod and Trinket are in the lead, I take off after them, trying to find trails that go in the same direction as the hounds. The fox and hounds run through property where we don't have permission to ride, and the huntsman and I set off in opposite directions to ride around the interdicted farm.

There's no trail on my side and my horse canters through the trees, sparing my knees somehow but ripping the sleeve of my heavy melton coat. I'm reminded of a scene in one of the Star Wars movies where the chasers and the chased dodge trees on flying motor scooters. We look for a gap in a wire fence and end up jumping a locked gate. The hounds are headed for the road and there could be a bad situation if one of us doesn't get there to stop them or the traffic.

When I reach the road, I hear the huntsman blowing "Gone to Ground." The hounds have safely crossed the road and put the fox to earth. When I find the huntsman, the hounds are barking proudly and trying to dig the fox out. From inside the tunnel comes the muffled bark of Playful, who is almost small enough to crawl down to the den. Nimrod is digging excitedly -- after all, it was his fox.

In a few minutes, the master and what's left of the field ride up. We recount the run, report on what individual hounds did and pull out our flasks. Finally, the huntsman calls the hounds off and we hack back to the vans in high spirits, leaving the fox to give us another run another day.

It seems now that the temperature has gone up a degree or two.

Back home, having cleaned my horse and turned him out to roll, I gratefully peel off my too-tight muddy boots. My neck is chafed from four hours in a tightly-tied stock and my muscles are tired from working hard in the cold. But those are good sensations that add up to the satisfaction of having done something on a gray wintry day.

The only thing is, now I have to make my own chili.

CHAPTER 34

'Yes Ma'am,' The Manners Police Are Desperately Needed by Today's Children

I've been trying to hold this in, but it is bugging me beyond belief. At the risk of insulting a lot of people, I have to ask: Is there anyone left who correctly uses the words "lie" and "lay"? Besides me, I mean.

For a long time my pet peeve was the use of "them" or "their" in reference to a singular antecedent. Example: "At one time or another, every child cuts their hair."

The feminists have made us all so gender sensitive that we are afraid to utter any word that has the remotest connotation of masculinity. So we have to butcher the language to keep from saying, "At one time or another, every child cuts his hair." It's perfectly clear to me that female children are included in this observation, not only because "his" can be taken to mean "his or her," but because my very own female child did in fact cut her own hair. Big time. Now she looks like my very own male child.

Up until January of this year, our short-haired child, Katie Bo, was under the almost exclusive influence of her parents, Cricket and me. And, although she was only four years old, she used "lie" and "lay" correctly. In the last five months, she has developed a life of her own, going to nursery school, attending camp, doing lunch with friends, etc. And the word "lie" has disappeared from her vocabulary.

She says things like, "I'm going to lay down on the fabric sofa." Then I shriek at her, "Lie! Lie! Lie! I'm going to *lie* on the fabric sofa." She looks at me in alarm and says, "No, *you* lay on the *green* sofa."

Cricket and I are having a similar problem teaching her to say "yes ma'am" and "yes sir." We correct her a thousand times every day. We offer her a piece of bubble gum and a gold star for each time she says it without being prompted. We beg babysitters and relatives to be "manners police."

Does it work? No.

The problem is that Katie Bo does not hear anyone else say "ma'am" and "sir" and "lie." None of her little friends, as far as I can tell, is being taught to say "ma'am" and "sir." (Maybe their parents have become as discouraged as we are and have given up.) And teachers don't reinforce the courtesy as they used to. And television...well, put it this way: If the Teen-age Mutant Ninja Turtles said "ma'am" and "sir," every child in America would have beautiful manners. (This is not a slam on TMNT, which is one of the few cartoons we let Katie Bo watch.)

Of course, failing to say "ma'am" and "sir" and using "lie" and "lay" incorrectly will not cause Katie Bo to grow up into a warped human being, although it may drive me to distraction. The really troubling thing about all this is what is says about parental influence on children vs. outside influence. Not only are outside influences stronger, they are at cross-purposes with parental goals.

Twenty-five years ago, society reinforced the teachings of parents, whether the issue was courteous address of adults or the advisability of chastity before marriage. Other parents, teachers, bus drivers, coaches and every adult who had contact with children told them to mind their manners and behave themselves.

There was a collective sense of responsibility for raising children.

When I was 12 or 13, I spent a week at the beach with my friend's family. The family matriarch, "Gonghee," took it as her duty to correct the manners of any child in sight, blood relative or not.

My parents were sticklers for good table manners, and I know they were pleased when Gonghee reinforced their teachings by giving me a lesson in how to butter bread: "Butter each piece as you hold the bread on the butter plate," she explained. That someone besides Momma and Daddy would make an issue of table manners made a big impression on me.

Virginia Wiley, my 12th-grade English teacher, was another adult who felt it was her duty to help youngsters along the way to being mannerly and well-spoken. She called her students "ladies" and "gentlemen," and she got respect, hard work and "yes ma'am" in return (not to mention the undying gratitude of her students' parents).

How am I supposed to teach my daughter to respect adults when every adult she meets encourages familiarity of the first-name, yeah-instead-of-yes-ma'am variety?

How am I supposed to teach my daughter not to use vulgar language when she hears a cartoon character say "butthead"? Or worse, when she hears "nice" people use four-letter words?

How am I supposed to teach my daughter modesty when anatomically correct terms are bandied about the classroom like multiplication tables?

How am I supposed to teach my daughter premarital sex is wrong when the government pays unwed mothers to have babies and most movie stars have at least one illegitimate child?

If, because of the insidious influence of society, Cricket and I cannot inculcate our child with something as simple as addressing adults as "ma'am" and "sir," how can we ever hope to keep her virginal and drug free until adult maturity takes over?

The world needs more Gonghees and Virginia Wileys, more adults willing to correct children's grammar and manners, more adults willing to make an issue of standards.

C H A P T E R   3 5

While We're on the Subject of Boats...

I grew up in Lynchburg, in the foothills of the Blue Ridge, which, before the construction of Smith Mountain Lake, was not your prime boating region. Neither one of my parents had any interest in boats of any description, although they once crossed the Atlantic on the Ile de France.

When my Uncle Dick became interested in sailing in the late 1950s and bought a sailboat, it was politely viewed as aberrant behavior by my parents. As we trundled up and down U. S. Route 29 with a horse trailer every weekend, my parents shook their heads in disbelief that anyone would want to do something as ridiculous as fool with a boat.

This attitude was reinforced during a summer vacation with friends in Maine. One evening we all got in the friends' motorboat and motored to a nearby village for a dockside dinner of lobster. On the way home in the dark, my daddy was somewhat horrified when we struck a log out in the ocean.

We got home safely but Daddy was deeply shaken. The next day the friends proposed a 50-mile run up the coast to Nova Scotia or somewhere. Privately, my daddy would sooner have swum to Nova Scotia than ride in his friend's boat again, but he didn't want to be so rude as to say so. So when the friend kept saying, "Come on, Bo, it'll be fun," Daddy finally said, "But I don't want to have that much fun."

This friend had a knack for provoking Daddy into profound remarks. On the same visit -- this is Maine, remember -- the host and his family were all going swimming off the rocks by their oceanfront house. They wanted Daddy to join them, but the frigid North Atlantic held no attrac-

1 6 3

tion as a swimming hole for my South Carolina daddy. As they continued to press him to join them, he finally burst out, "Hell, I don't even drink water that cold!"

When my older brother, Bo, took to hanging around with Uncle Dick and reading books about sailing, my parents began to view boating with a kinder eye. Bo became serious enough about the water to work on a series of ships of questionable seaworthiness, which temporarily dampened Momma and Daddy's newfound enthusiasm for boating.

Then Bo bought and worked a shrimp boat in South Carolina for some weary time, which dampened his enthusiasm for boating, too.

Somewhere along the line, Daddy became disenchanted with pulling a horse trailer up and down U.S. Route 29, possibly because the highway was perpetually under construction, but also possibly because he was tired of throwing all his money away on horses. It occurred to him that he could spare himself the trouble of driving up and down U.S. Route 29 and still throw all his money away if he just had a boat.

So he bought an old wooden Matthews that he aptly named "Frustration."

In the last 10 years, he and Momma have spent all their spare time working on "the boat" and, once or twice, have actually left the dock for a short spin around Urbanna Creek. Daddy has all the comforts of home on "the boat," including air conditioning, heat, microwave, telephone, etc., plus all sorts of sophisticated navigational and communication equipment. He says he could go to Europe if he could just find a long enough extension cord.

"Frustration" is no longer "the boat," of course. He has traded up and down and bought and sold boats the way he used to trade horses and they way he still trades cars.

The last few boats he has bought were all tied up in Florida marinas when he bought them. Since they don't ship ships UPS, he has had to go to Florida to bring the new boat back up the coast to Virginia. My Uncle Dick has run up and down the Inland Waterway in his sailboat for years, so Daddy figured there was nothing to it.

Of course, Daddy, a horseman-come-lately to boating, figured there was nothing to it because he had an ace in the hole: my brother Bo.

After a lengthy spell of working on commercial vessels with sieves as hulls, Bo eventually found employment on a seaworthy vessel. He is a tugboat captain and a first class waterman.

Daddy thought anybody who could find and lasso a loose barge on the Chesapeake Bay during a winter storm at night could pilot a yacht up the Inland Waterway. So Daddy invited Bo and a few unsuspecting friends to join him on the trip north with a boat named "Sundog."

It was hideously hot, and Daddy didn't have a long enough extension cord, so there was no air conditioning and no power for the refrigerator. Everyone on board had a schedule to make, so they drove hard up the coast. By the time they got to Virginia, they all looked like castaways who had been rescued after 137 days of floating around without showers, shade or razor blades.

Men like being grubby, so the trip was a big success. So much so that the next year, when Daddy bought another boat in Florida, the original crew was eager to help bring it north. The new boat had a generator, though, which meant they had power while they were underway. The availability of showers, air conditioning and electric razors detracted greatly from the pleasure of the trip, I understand.

This latest model has been renamed "Dockside" in deference to reality. Actually, Daddy likes to take the boat for a cruise out to Buoy Six on the Rappahannock, but getting the boat untied and out of the slip is such a huge undertaking that he seldom makes the effort.

For one thing, he has such a complex arrangement of lines holding the boat in its slip that it takes a well-coordinated and obedient crew of 12 to untie the boat at the precise moment he hollers that he's ready to back it out. For another, he'd rather spend all day down in the bottom of the boat with the engine (and the air conditioner) than cruising around the river in the sunshine.

As a leitmotif of boat ownership, Momma and Daddy are always talking about dinghies. Ever since Momma realized, eight or nine years ago, that Daddy was never going to have enough crew to cast off the lines and leave the dock, she has wanted a dinghy to play around in in Urbanna Creek.

One day Daddy found a small wooden dinghy on shore and bought it for $50, oars included. Momma was delighted, and they immediately put it in the water. Daddy maneuvered the dinghy over next to the boat and Momma climbed down.

The dinghy had no centerboard and was sort of wishy-washy, so when Momma stepped down into it, it slipped sideways and she fell in the water. Clothed, of course.

She waded ashore and Daddy rowed around to the beach, where she tried again. She got in the dinghy all right, but with the weight of two people in it, the water was lapping at the gunwales.

Daddy had rowed gently out to the middle of the creek before they noticed April, their Labrador retriever, dog-paddling furiously after them. Momma said later Daddy acted just like Jimmy Carter with the killer rabbit. He hollered at her to chase the dog away with an oar.

"If she gets near us, she'll swamp the boat!"

Momma, who was already wet, was less perturbed at the prospect of a swim.

Somehow they outran the dog, rowing furiously back to shore. As Daddy said when they beached the boat, "Well, I've already had $50 worth of fun with this dinghy."

That was the only time they took the dinghy out. The oars lay around until they got lost, and Daddy finally sold it. "Sundog" came with a dinghy on davits, but that was too complicated to fool with.

"Dockside" came with one of those fancy inflatable, motorized dinghies, but Momma has always had an uneasy feeling that putting a motor on a large inner tube will sink it.

Recently Momma told me they had bought another $50 dinghy. This one has a sail and, more important, a centerboard. And the dog doesn't want to get in it.

CHAPTER 36

Summer Olympics Need Dessert to Go with Entrée

I f NBC is scratching its corporate head trying to figure out why ratings of its coverage of the summer Olympics were so poor, the network need look no further than the Olympic menu itself. Where is the cheesecake? Where is the strawberry shortcake with mounds of whipped cream? Where are the cherries jubilee, the crêpes flambé?

In the winter Olympics, that's where.

The problem with the summer Olympics is that they are all meat and potatoes, all muscle and sweat and sinew. For 17 days and nights, viewers see nothing but half-naked bodies with bulging muscles glistening with sweat. The cameras zoom in on every well-defined biceps, triceps and quadriceps.

The 100-meter sprints are shown over and over in slow motion so viewers can see the well-oiled works of human running machines like Carl Lewis and Florence Griffith Joyner. Scantily-clad swimmers and gymnasts display beautifully developed deltoids as they compete. And weight lifters give anatomy lessons with every jerk as their muscles pop out in relief.

The summer Olympics are indisputably athletic.

The winter games, on the other hand, are three parts entertainment and spectacle for every two parts athletic competition. To start with, nobody in the winter Olympics sweats. Even if they did, who could tell under their clothes?

The figure skaters wear fabulous, frilly costumes. The skiers wear brilliant, crisply colored snow suits. The speed skaters wear sleek skins with bold patterns. Even the biathletes sport an interesting look with their rifles slung over their backs.

And all that gay coloring is set against a background of white snow or ice. When the cameramen get the lighting right, it makes a gorgeous, clean picture.

Compare that to a screenful of sweaty track shorts.

Florence Griffith Joyner was NBC's only hope for an athlete as colorful as its peacock, but evidently she was asked/required to wear the American uniform.

Not that Flo-Jo didn't look good in that red leotard, but think how exciting it would have been to see her streaking away from the field wearing one-legged tights, a multi-colored leotard and streamers in her hair, as she did at the Olympic Trials. She really is in a different class and she should be allowed to wear the trappings of individuality that are justly hers. Plus, NBC could have used the extra three ratings points.

With Flo-Jo out of the running, the winter Olympics also win the competition for weirdest sporting attire. Nothing in the summer games compares with the bodysuit lugers wear that keeps their feet pointed and makes walking impossible. The winter games get the silver medal in weird attire, too, for the bulky, shapeless uniform and Halloween mask worn by ice hockey goalies.

The summer games lose out in other categories of entertainment value, too. The drama just wasn't there this time. The announcers gave a big build-up to the US-USSR men's basketball game, in which the US was supposed to avenge a loss in Munich in 1972. However, the US lost in a major upset.

For American viewers, that wasn't nearly as dramatic as when the upset went the other way, the "Lake Placid Miracle" in ice hockey in 1980. Who could forget America's young goalie Mike Eruzione making save after save against the seasoned Soviets?

Several fine American athletes won multiple golds in 1984 without the Soviet bloc countries and wanted to repeat the feat (a) this time against the whole world and (b) because no one had ever repeated. That should have been dramatic, but doing something marvelous the second time is never as exciting as the first time.

Greg Louganis is the exception here. The winner of gold medals in springboard and platform diving at Los Angeles, he was expected to win again in Seoul. But the finest diver probably in the history of the world did something every viewer (and every diver) fears: During the springboard competition, he hit his head on the diving board.

In an incredible display of guts, Louganis returned to the competition with his head stitched up and made difficult, precise dives to win the gold medal. In the platform competition, winning the gold came down to his last dive, which had to be perfect, which it was.

The man has ice water in his veins.

Another problem with the Seoul games was that everybody had the same name. The men in track and field were all named Lewis and the women were all named Joyner. The gymnasts were all named Nadia or Svetlana.

Also, several individuals seemed to be hogging all the medals. I don't think it's really cricket for American swimmer Matt Biondi to win seven gold medals. Three or four ought to be enough for anybody. Biondi shouldn't feel compelled to make up the difference between the American and Soviet medal count all by himself.

The heart of the ratings problem for NBC, though, was the fact that there is no event in the summer Olympics comparable to ice skating. Ice skating, unlike every other event in the summer and winter Olympics, is entertainment.

Sure, there are elements of sport, in the athletic sense of the word, to ice dancing and figure skating, but Olympic level ice skating goes beyond pure sport. It combines music, dance, color, strength and agility into a competitive pageant that attracts record audiences night after night after night.

Significantly, ice dancing and figure skating are the only Olympic sports whose professional version is purely entertainment. Tai Babalonia, Peggy Fleming, Scott Hamilton, all those performer-athletes move on to professional touring ice shows after they win medals.

In the summer games, the only sport that comes close to having the entertainment value of figure skating is gymnastics.

Here, 12-year-old nymphs with double-jointed spines and legs that start just below their armpits prance, twist, leap and flip through the air in ways that simply defy gravity. These children are entertaining to watch, but without Mary Lou Retton and a chance for a medal this year, the competition wasn't quite as riveting.

One American gymnast was 21 years old and married! No wonder the US didn't win a medal in gymnastics. Gymnasts are not even supposed to have bras, much less husbands.

Most of all, the summer games were missing Eddie the Eagle. You remember him, the truly amateur ski jumper who skied down the 90 meter jump and then fell like a stone when he got to the end. Despite a pathetic showing, he holds the British record for the ski jump, mainly because he's the only Englishman ever to do it in official competition.

He was a sensation at Calgary last winter because he was the best example of what the Olympics are supposed to be about: the pure joy of participation.

The summer games athlete who reminds me most of Eddie the Eagle is, oddly enough, the best in the world at what she does, Florence Griffith Joyner. When she bursts off the starting line at light speed and then, in the stretch, shifts to warp speed, Joyner gives the impression of running for the pure joy of running. For sheer beauty and the essence of Olympics competition, it's hard to beat the sight of Flo Jo sprinting into history faster than any woman has ever run before.

That should have been worth 25 rating points right there.

CHAPTER 37

The Mysterious Schedule of 'Subs'

J ust in case you've ever spent any time wondering what it would be like to live on a construction site, I want to assure you it's nonstop fun and games. Right. To survive, you definitely have to have a sense of humor and a great faith in the ability of your lawn to regenerate itself.

One thing that makes life-under-construction bearable, even fun, is having workmen who are as nice and lively as the men working on our addition.

They're more than halfway done now. They've pretty much finished the exterior and they're ready to demolish the wall separating the old part of the house from the new.

This project started out to be a private bathroom for our second-story bedroom. Then we realized we'd have to put something under the bathroom to hold it up, so we decided to enlarge the kitchen. Pretty soon the enlarged kitchen became a kitchen-family room with fireplace and adjoining terrace.

Then we had a lot more room on the second floor than we needed for a bathroom, so we designed closets, a dressing area and a marvelous aerie where I will be inspired to compose extraordinarily brilliant prose that will command great sums of money to pay for all this construction work.

We had some plans drawn and we have followed one or two aspects of the plans faithfully. Otherwise, this has been a design-as-you-build project. What that means is the supervisor knocks on the back door eight or nine times a day and says, "Mrs. Williams, could you come out here a minute and tell us where you want the thusandsuch?"

So I cart the baby out there and make executive decisions about the size of the windows, whether the French doors will be finished or painted, how high the raised hearth will be and what the steps to the patio will look like. It makes me wonder how people do this when they work full time.

Our contractor does beautiful work, but there are unpredictable setbacks in every construction job. The very first day of our project, one of the men turned a horse loose. The supervisor had asked me if they could park the backhoe trailer in the pasture, which I said was fine. I didn't see the trailer anywhere among the 45 trucks parked in our driveway, so I assumed he was going to bring it another day.

Five minutes after I left to do errands, the trailer fell out of the sky and they decided to park it in the pasture. Accordingly, one of the men opened the gate and started to drive the trailer through.

Mele, a middle-aged broodmare, was standing nearby. Mele looks half asleep most of the time, but this is a ruse to disguise the fact that she is waiting for someone to open the gate three or four inches so she can escape.

As the workman drove slowly through the gate, Mele passed him going the other way at a high rate of speed.

Whenever Mele gets out, which is embarrassingly often, she gallops down Lee Road, past Betty Swindler's barn to Contention. Betty has caught Mele so many times that she doesn't get excited anymore when Mele gallops past. *Well, there goes Mele again.*

On this particular day, Betty was standing in front of her barn and, in her words, "I saw Mele go flying past with a dump truck in hot pursuit."

Betty came to the rescue of both Mele and the guilt-ridden workman, catching the mare and leading her home.

The next day, the workmen cut the septic line, but we expected that because nobody knew where it was in the first place. Then they tore up the slate walk so the cement truck wouldn't crush it when they poured the footings. And then the supervisor put little signs all over the back yard saying "sand," "bricks" and so on.

After that, we went through a period of several weeks during which there was a lot of activity but nobody did any work. Every day, giant trucks with cranes drove in the driveway to test how far the branches of the trees would bend before breaking.

The cranes would unload building materials in the back yard. The drivers would always ask me where I wanted the lumber or the bricks or the shingles, and I would point to whatever patch of grass remained unoccupied. Then they would have me sign a piece of paper signifying they had unloaded something in our back yard.

Building materials don't have names. They go strictly by numbers. So I signed pieces of paper attesting that we had received 11 29-47x59s and 156 units of 3(10)-75.4 and 15 44x56, 8/1s.

Pretty soon, the whole back yard, the side yard and part of the driveway were full of building materials. We had big squares of bricks, stacks of cinder blocks, piles of plywood, rolls of tarpaper, bundles of shingles, heaps of sand, hundreds of board feet of assorted lumber -- and no workmen.

Every now and then, the supervisor would drive by and ask if the windows had been delivered yet.

Once, three of the workmen I recognized drove in and I got all excited as they unloaded another pile of cinder blocks. Then they took two ladders and drove away.

The scheduling of construction crews is a deep mystery, revealed only to licensed contractors who swear eternal oaths not to tell homeowners. Whatever the truth may be, the contractors blame the on-again, off-again nature of their scheduling on "the subs."

"The subs" have their own mysterious scheduling system. The heart of this system is to arrange their work so they never complete a job all at once.

For instance, the roofer has come three times. The first time was 6 p.m. on a Friday, when he and his helper said they were going to put the roof on the wing. However, they had forgotten something called a "ladderator," which hauls the shingles up the ladder to the roof, so they couldn't work as fast.

The next morning they came back with the ladderator and worked until the roofer's helper gashed his arm on his shingle knife. They came back from the emergency room later that same afternoon and worked till dark without finishing. That was three weeks ago.

The plumber comes for an hour or two every now and then and drills holes in the joists. The electrician comes and writes on the studs. The heating/air conditioning people have made numerous visits, but they haven't finished, either.

Eventually the regular workmen came back, this time in droves. "The subs" were here, too, and one crazy day there must have been 25 men working. The noise from hammers, saws, compressors and mortar-mixers was incredible.

The electrician and his helper were there, and they asked me to climb up the ladder to the second floor and discuss light switches and outlets.

The baby was in the playpen in the hall, crying intermittently. The air conditioning workmen stopped and consoled her on their many trips back and forth to the attic, where they were cutting holes in the bedroom ceilings with a jack hammer.

The phone rang frequently and one of the workmen on the ground kept hollering up to me, "Mrs. Williams, do you want me to get that?"

The plumber and two or three other men were standing in line to ask me what to do about all the stuff that goes in the walls or under the crawl space.

In between making all these executive decisions, I was trying to finish writing a column. At that very moment, the air conditioning people wanted to cut a hole in the ceiling directly over my computer and dump plaster dust all over it. So I hollered up the attic steps, "I'm almost done! Just give me 15 more minutes!"

They did, but they thought it was poor scheduling.

CHAPTER 38

The Animals Have Us Well-Trained

For a week now we've been tiptoeing out the back door all hunched over so as not to disturb the wren that is nesting on the top shelf on the back porch. She is brooding four eggs, as near as I can tell. Wrens build fabulous nests, fit to outlast Armageddon. And they do it in about two days, too.

They bring great hanks of oak feathers, which are in abundance this time of year, and layer them with dead oak leaves and other non-biodegradable materials until they have a sort of hive about eight inches high. In front there is a small entrance, a tunnel really, that goes back and down into the hive.

So the eggs are out of sight and the wren, when she is sitting on them, can rest her chin on her doorsill and keep watch.

The mother-to-be on our back porch built her bunker on a basket of gardening things. Luckily, I'm too busy to do much gardening right now anyway.

This is her second nest. She started one a few weeks ago and I threw it out before it was completely fortified. Cricket, my husband, and I conscientiously kept the screen door shut for a week or so, hoping the nesting urge would drive the wren to build elsewhere. But she had her heart set on our porch and that was that. By the time we noticed the second nest, it was too late.

So now, for two more weeks while she sits and then two or three more weeks until her babies fledge, we'll have to keep the screen door open. This is not a great hardship. It just means if we open the back door to get some air, we'll have to take the flies, too.

I'm making an effort to use one of the other doors to keep from driving the wren off her nest unnecessarily. If I sort of sneak in and out and avoid eye contact, she stays put. But if I look at her or pause to change my muddy shoes, she darts out and flies to the dogwood tree. Cricket has grumbled a bit about being dive-bombed every morning when he leaves for work, but I think we'll all make it through gestation.

I am a little worried about four baby wrens learning to fly on the back porch with three cats lying on the stoop.

There is another wren in the neighborhood who likes to nest in our paper box. Every year as soon as I notice the globs of oak hair and leaves in the box, I hang a basket and a sign on the box for the delivery man: "Nesting wren." He respects motherhood, too.

Birds are not the only creatures I try to accommodate.

Cats are especially adept at arranging for people to go out of their way on their behalf. My old blond cat, Flynn, had me well trained. He spent a lot of time outdoors, hunting and traveling a surprising distance. But when I walked to the end of the drive to get the paper, he wanted me to carry him. So I did.

When Cricket and I moved into this house, we had a beloved old dog who liked to sleep by our bed. Rally was getting frail and had trouble with slick floors and smooth steps. The steps in the house had individual braided rugs stapled to them. The rugs were old, impossible to clean and not my taste to begin with. But we left them in place for three years so Rally could climb the stairs to bed.

My mother is the same way. Daddy says Momma is so foolish about animals that he's going to have a bumper sticker made for her that reads: "I Brake for Butterflies."

Her cats have her trained, too. The finicky eating habits of cats are legendary. Why do you think they make cat food with names like Gourmet and Fancy Feast?

Occasionally, an animal will push too far.

Momma had some cat she was trying to coax a few calories into, so she bought these eentsy-teentsy cans of hummingbird tongues or some such delicacy. But of course the cat wouldn't eat but a teaspoonful at a sitting, so Momma wrapped up the can and put it in the refrigerator for the next meal.

"But then the cat wouldn't eat it because it was cold," she told me. "So one day I found myself fixing a plate of cat food and putting it in the microwave. That's when I switched to dry food and told the cat he could eat it or starve."

CHAPTER 39

From Here to Maternity

I had the mare bred last month, over Cricket's protests. She's a nice mare, and she has a handsome, athletic colt, now three years old, so it seemed like a good thing to do.

But Cricket can be excused for wondering why we're going through that ordeal again. To start with, he thinks we already have too many horses, which is true. But I think his concern runs deeper than that. After all, he's been involved with several maternal emergencies on my account, and every time things have gone awry.

Attending the birth of another living thing is an unparalleled experience, but, as the cruise ships advertise, getting there is half the fun.

The last time this mare had a foal, she was two weeks late. I got up at two-hour intervals every night for weeks to check on her, until I began hallucinating from lack of sleep. She finally foaled one Friday afternoon about an hour before our houseguests and their four children arrived for the weekend.

It took two big strong men, Tom Newton and Cricket, to pull the foal into the world, and then it took until 3:30 in the morning for us to convince the mare it was OK to let her baby nurse.

All of which failed to prepare Cricket for the birth of our daughter. He didn't deliver her but he did get me to the hospital so Dr. Lewis Williams could deliver her. It was supposed to be a scheduled delivery, but who really believes that will happen? I came home from the doctor's office on Tuesday with the news that he wanted me to meet him at the hospital at 6:30 the following morning.

We were both excited, but our excitement took different forms.

Cricket wanted to sit on the porch and discuss the cosmic aspects of parenthood. I wanted to water the houseplants, fold the laundry, pack my bag and fix the windows in case it rained while I was gone.

Fortunately, Michael Babb came over and entertained Cricket. What they did was entertain themselves through a good portion of a bottle of scotch. We finally went to bed at midnight, and Cricket had been asleep at least 30 minutes before I went into labor.

He was completely disoriented when I tried to wake him up. "This is not right. We're not supposed to go to the hospital till 6:30," he said as he fumbled with his clothes. "I thought this was supposed to be planned childbirth."

He took my bag and got in the car to wait for me to water a few more houseplants. On the drive in, I timed my contractions. Every time I asked Cricket to turn on the interior light so I could look at my watch, he pressed harder on the accelerator. As it turned out, we got to the hospital with a mere eight hours to spare, eight hours during which Cricket paced up and down the halls smoking cigarettes and discovering that he had left his wallet at home.

Cricket's collaboration with me on maternal emergencies began in 1983 with a bizarre attempt to see someone we didn't even know have a baby. I was working as a reporter for a major metropolitan newspaper at the time.

When photographer Tommy Price and I arranged with a local mid-wife to let us cover a home delivery (childbirth, not milk), she warned us that getting there could be a problem. It took three frantic trips before we hit it right, but the dry run one February night was the most memorable.

The two couples we had interviewed beforehand live in the two most inaccessible places for a Goochlander: the huge, planned neighborhood south of the river called Brandermill and the two-counties distant rural community of Old Church. And we all know babies elect to come at the most inconvenient times. So it should have been no surprise when the first husband called at 11 p.m. and said, "Come to Brandermill."

The only way to get to Brandermill from our house, short of going to North Carolina first, is to slip across the State Farm bridge and go through Powhatan Correctional Center. I was packing my gun and my dog for the expedition when Cricket decided to escort me.

Despite the nobility of his gesture, I would say that night was one of the least romantic in our marriage. We had both worked late and neither one of us had had supper. I had a cold. None of the vehicles had any gas. And we argued all the way to Brandermill. He didn't want me wandering around the prison by myself in the middle of the night, and I questioned what he was going to do for three-five-nine hours while this baby got birthed.

We arrived shortly after midnight, threading our way through the maze of Brandermill streets with a map. Cricket said he was going to buy gas and then sleep in the front seat till I was ready to go.

When I went into the house, there was a whole crowd of people to view the birth: friends and neighbors, the assistant midwife and Tommy Price with all his camera gear. I found this totally bizarre, but then I'm not the sort of person who feels it's a gesture of love to share your bodily functions with friends.

Ten minutes later, the midwife came downstairs and announced that it was false labor and she was going home and go back to bed. After she left, Tommy said he might as well go on home, too. Then the friends and neighbors departed, and the couple went upstairs to bed.

Embarrassed that I couldn't leave, I sat by the window with the assistant midwife, who was staying over. She entertained me with her life story and then her husband's life story (He was a child psychologist and took care of Larry Hagman's daughter when he was in California but now he was with the city schools but he really wanted to be a sheet metal worker but that didn't pay enough and she was his fourth and last wife).

Meanwhile, Cricket was having a strange conversation with the woman clerk at the gas station, who wanted him to chase away a guy who was hiding behind the building and who kept coming out and flashing her.

When he got back to Brandermill, he realized he didn't have any idea where the house was or what the couple's name was. So he drove up and down streets for awhile, hoping I would come out and flag him down. Then he went to a bar on Rt. 360 and called some friends who live in Brandermill.

By then it was 2:30 a.m. and he was waking people up with: "Hi, this is Cricket. I've lost my wife. She's birthing a baby in Brandermill."

They thought it was one of his pranks but they let him come over anyway. Then, after a few wrong numbers, he got a hold of Tommy Price, who had been home in bed for two hours by then. Tommy gave Cricket the address and Cricket rescued me just as I was fixing to throttle the assistant midwife.

We drove back across the State Farm bridge with Cricket swearing he'd never go on another assignment with me again.

The next morning, the woman in Brandermill had her baby but Tommy and I missed it. About a week later, the phone rang at 4 a.m. The woman in Old Church was in labor. I jumped up and pulled on some clothes, but Cricket didn't even roll over.

"Take the gun," was all he said.

CHAPTER 40

'Cooking' Is a Term to Be Used Loosely

Adding onto your house is like having a big wedding. If you knew ahead of time how it would discombobulate your life, you'd never dream of doing it.

At this point, I'm so sick of the project that I would gladly return to the old kitchen and single bathroom if the workmen could put everything back the way it was by 4:30 this afternoon. Mary Lamb Lucas lived with her entire house in ruins for more than a year, and Rossie Fisher will celebrate the first anniversary of life on a jobsite next month. Women of great fortitude, those two.

I've suffered only three months but that's long enough.

No matter how wonderful the new wing will be when it's born, I'll always have strong memories of the labor and delivery.

On July 8, the day they took my kitchen out, we had a dinner party on the bricks. There were big cubes of bricks sitting around the back yard, and we dressed one of them up as a buffet table. We covered it with a linen tablecloth, put out candelabra and silverware and set a flower arrangement in the middle.

But the novelty wore off on July 9. I'm tired of preparing meals on the floor like a hut dweller. At the low point, I had to thread my way through stacks of kitchen cabinets and crawl under the kitchen table on my hands and knees to get the magic biscuits out of the toaster oven. It was the only way to spread out all the appliances so they weren't on the same circuit.

Cricket put up a card table in the dining room and arranged the electric frying pan, the toaster oven and the hot plate on it. The microwave oven is nearby on the sideboard. It's a very workable arrangement -- as long as you don't want to use more than one appliance at a time.

One night I was heating oil in the electric frying pan and cooking vegetables in the microwave oven when the fuse blew. With the baby in my arms, I groped my way along the dark hall and down into the basement and found the breaker box. As soon as I got back upstairs, I put the baby's bottle in the microwave and blew the darn thing again.

Sometimes that happens three or four times during the preparation of one meal. (I'm a slow learner.)

Kay Higgins, who went through this ordeal some years ago herself, kindly loaned us her hot plate. However, the hot plate has wearied of front line duty and it only heats half-heartedly.

That hasn't kept me from burning up three pans on it, though. I'd put a pan of snaps on and think, Oh, it'll take an hour to boil. Next thing you know, there's a blackened pan with unidentifiable glop bonded to the metal.

I was in the grocery store last week when I realized that my attempts at cooking without a kitchen had reached their nadir. I had gone down three or four aisles in tandem with a fellow in jeans, pausing at the same shelves he did, when at last he spoke.

"We must cook the same way because we're buying the same things," he observed cheerfully.

So it's come to this, I thought, I'm cooking on the level of a young bachelor.

We couldn't have built this wing on our house without the green ruler. I have this wooden green ruler which I used to draw our plans on graph paper and with which the supervisor and I have measured cabinets, windowsills, door jambs, step risers and every conceivable facet of the project. We'd be standing there eyeing a closet opening, trying to determine how high the shelves should be, and I'd say, "Well, how far above that bracket can we go?"

The supervisor would pat his hip, feeling for a tape measure. Finding none, he'd say, "Where's the green ruler?"

CHAPTER 41

Memories I Can Do Without, #385 --Fly Paper.

Back in June, the supervisor kept talking about getting the wing "closed up tight" and he carefully locked all the windows and doors when the men left each evening. As soon as he left, I opened them back up again, because, as hot as it was this summer, the wing would have exploded if it had stayed "closed up tight" for more than 30 minutes.

What this meant was that every fly and flying creature in Crozier came through the wing. Because I was "cooking" in there, many of the flying creatures stayed in there to keep me company, although a few went into the dining room, also a "cooking" area.

One day in desperation I bought half a dozen fly strips at Southern States. Never have I had a worse idea.

I hung one strip from the light in the kitchen and one from the chandelier in the dining room. Both of them exceeded all expectations in snaring flies. In two days we had a truly amazing assortment of flying creatures hanging from the light fixtures in both rooms.

The reason fly strips work so well is that they use the same powerful glue used in television ads to show how you can pick up a truck with one drop. This is fine when you're catching flies or picking up trucks, but it is a drawback when you get your hair caught, which I did every single time I walked through the dining room, which was 542 times every day.

By the time we took the fly strips down, I had to shave my head to get the glue-encrusted hair off.

Flies aren't the only ones to come in through the wing.

Our pets quickly found the doors in the wing, which stay open most of the time. We not only have half the flies in Goochland in the house, we have cats and dogs coming and going all day and night, mostly coming. As soon as I put a dog out the back door, he runs around the house to the wing doors. Most times he beats me back to the living room.

Then there was the rainy day that men and dogs tracked red clay all through the house. Every time I heard a door open, I'd holler, "Don't let the dog in." Just about then, Pigtail would trot into the living room on muddy paws.

For awhile there was a ditch in the kitchen floor between the old part and the new. It went down to the crawl space and I swept the dirt and sawdust into it every evening. The cats discovered it, and I was frequently taken aback as a cat materialized in the middle of the kitchen floor.

The workmen know the names of all the cats and dogs and speak kindly and familiarly to each animal every time one appears. Poor Pigtail, our German shepherd and former watchdog, is terminally confused by the situation. After guarding the top of the steps for the first few months and having me call her aside to let a stream of strange people go into our bedroom, she has given up. She is now utterly worthless as a watchdog.

On the bright side, the project has done wonders for my resolve to get up early. I'm always jumping up at 6:45 and jerking on some clothes just before the workmen begin trooping through our bedroom or the painters begin peeping through the windows. If I oversleep, I have to crawl around under the windowsills until I get dressed.

It isn't just early morning when our privacy is compromised. We went through one lengthy period during which the contractor stationed a carpenter, a roofer or a painter at every bathroom window from 7 a.m. to 4 p.m., Monday through Friday.

At times the workmen seem like part of the household. The supervisor is always meeting me at the back door as I return from the barn and saying, "Mrs. Williams, your baby was crying so I gave her the bottle she'd thrown on the floor." Or, "Mrs. Williams, your butter beans were burning, so I turned them off." Or giving me all my phone messages (after I give them all of theirs.)

They're moving right along these days, spurred no doubt by my threats of writing more columns, and I'm quite sure they'll be done and out of here by the turn of the century.

Lost in Time and Space
While Supper Burns

Katie Bo, 4, and I recently read two wonderful books about children in far different circumstances from hers. "Tar Beach" by Faith Ringgold is about a young girl in Harlem who has fantasies about flying while her family has a picnic on the roof of their apartment building. "Alistair in Outer Space" by Marilyn Sadler is about a little boy who is whisked away by aliens while trying to return books to the library.

Katie Bo had selected these books from the Goochland Library herself, after rejecting numerous others because "they don't have interesting pictures."

As we read them, I kept thinking to myself, she can't identify with these children. She won't enjoy these books.

But I was wrong. She is fascinated with both stories. At her request, we have read them over and over, discussing what the children are doing, what they are thinking and where they are. The result is that Katie Bo has probably categorized New York City and the planet of Gootula as equally far-fetched and imaginative places.

The value of that has finally come home to me. Firmly and unfortunately rooted in reality as I am these days, I remembered at last how wonderful it is to have so many different worlds available for exploration through the magic of reading.

The responsibilities of a family and a job give me little time to get lost in a book anymore, but I'm thankful for the many years I had to travel through the time machine of books. Reading has enabled me to be reincarnated as a noblewoman in the Tudor court and a cowpoke on the

Western frontier, to fight in the Revolutionary War, to live in "Inja" during the British Empire, to die hunting gold in the Yukon.

Living those many lives requires two things: books and the leisure to read them. For all practical purposes, then, time-travel through books is the delicious province of children and retirees.

You can't get lost in a book when you have grass to mow, crops to grow, deals to do or supper to fix. In fact, the last time I did get lost in a book, it almost ruined my life.

The book was Tom Wolfe's "Bonfire of the Vanities." I became so engrossed in that book that I walked around reading it, holding it before my eyes with one hand, feeding and changing the baby, cooking, weeding, ironing with the other. Some project came up and I finally had to send the book to my husband's office until I got done with the project.

I'd rather snatch at pieces of a book than not read at all, but to get into a book and live the life it offers, you must have hours at a time to read large chunks of it. It takes the sort of endless summer afternoons on which children are wont to say, "There's nothing to do." How I envy a bored child. I look at him and think, Here, you take my responsibilities (you won't be bored) and I'll take your leisure and read!

The power of a good book is almost physical. (The power of trash is, too: It moves me to throw it away. There are so many good, exciting books, I haven't time to waste on trash.)

All my life, my family has teased me about my tendency to become mesmerized by the written word. Whenever anything escapes my attention, someone will say, "Oh, Robin had her nose in a book." My husband says I cannot walk past the kitchen counter without pausing to read the newspaper. (It's true. Little tentacles reach up from the newsprint and grab my shirt collar if I try to walk past.)

Growing up, I went to bed with a book every night. My parents would call from their room, "Turn out the light. It's 10 (or 11 or 12) o'clock."

"Let me finish this chapter," I'd say. Or the ever-faithful, "Just one more page."

But each page led to the next fascinating page, and it was impossible for me to leave Tarzan in the clutches of the Ant Men when his faithful Waziri warriors were miles away in the jungle, ignorant of his fate.

I clearly remember the day my mother asked me to watch a pot of beans on the stove while she went outside to do some chore. I sat in the kitchen, not six feet from the stove, reading "White Fang." As I read, the life was slowly being choked out of the wolfdog by a pit bull that had him by the throat. White Fang twisted and jumped, slashing the pit bull's shoulder and flinging his body against the wall of the pen, but the pit bull hung on, grinding his teeth ever closer to White Fang's jugular with his stupendous jaws...

When Momma returned, the beans were burned, the pot melted and the kitchen filled with acrid, black smoke.

I had merely moved the book closer to my face to keep reading.

Getting to the Meat of the Story

his is an article about cows, but it begins with a story about chickens.

One of the all-time best parties I ever went to was a costume party our friends Mary and Julian had on April 15 one year. The date and Julian's occupation -- accountant -- provided the theme: taxes. Guests were to come dressed as their favorite charity or tax deduction.

The success of a costume party depends on the willingness of the guests to look foolish, and it turns out that Mary and Julian have a jolly lot of friends who will go to great lengths to look foolish. Most of the guests were quite clever. I remember someone came wearing a flowered shirt and carrying a brief case -- a business trip to Hawaii.

The prize, if I'd been awarding it, would have gone to Bill and Helen Scott Reed. Helen Scott, noted opera supporter, came as Brunhilda, complete with long gown, long braids and horned helmet. But Bill came as Helen Scott, complete with heels, dress and floppy hat. They were terrific.

Another one of the Reeds, Rossie Reed Fisher, was also innovative in her costume. Everyone would ask her why she had come as a chicken and she would correct each person: "I've come as my rooster, because the chickens aren't tax-deductible without the rooster."

It seems you have to have breeding stock in order to take a deduction on the maintenance of livestock.

Along the same lines (and this gives me the opportunity to segue into cows), Andy Shield came in a costume indicating his tax-deductible cattle. Not wishing to put on a "get up," as my mother would call it, Andy simply pinned to his shirt a round piece of cardboard painted brown and sporting a fly scotch-taped to it.

Andy has a serious herd of cows, enough cows to refer to them as cattle. I'm not sure where the numerical break point is between "cows" and "cattle," but it's certainly in double digits. You wouldn't refer to seven or eight bovines as "cattle" unless you were being facetious. Fifteen or twenty, though, probably qualify as "cattle."

Harvey Layne used to have "cattle," 175 head to be exact. Then he took sick three years ago and had to cut down. "Cows are high now," Harvey said recently. "I sold mine in the cheapest market there ever was, I reckon."

He has "cows" now, more specifically, two cows and a steer. The steer is six years old and, not being breeding stock, isn't tax deductible. The steer weighs around 1,200 pounds and would probably fetch a good price at the livestock market if anyone could catch him and get him there.

Harvey was talking about trying to tranquilize him and catch him. He didn't elaborate on how he planned to get the tranquilizer into the steer. Tranquilizer or no, catching a 1,200-pound steer that doesn't want to be caught is going to be a bit of a rodeo. If catching that steer is as good a show as the one-steer rodeo we had in our driveway a few years back, Harvey could probably sell tickets and make as much as the market price of the steer.

The rodeo we had started out as a cattle roundup, or more accurately, a calf roundup. At the time, David Johnson, my neighbor around the corner on Route 6, owned "cows": two black calves. He bought them and raised them for a year or two, and then I guess he either sold them or had them slaughtered.

(We're getting into the meat of the story now.)

One day the calves got out. It's important to understand that these "calves" weren't newborn leather pouches of adorability. They were more like 500-pound forklifts wheeling around without drivers.

David Johnson and his neighbors were able to persuade one of the calves to return to the pen, but the other one jogged east on Route 6 along the State Farm fence and disappeared.

The first I knew about it was when I saw a strange man in the driveway. It was a member of the Johnson clan. He wanted to know if I'd seen the calf. I had heard a calf bawling, but I had assumed it was one of the State Farm's cattle -- until I remembered the State Farm cattle hadn't been in the field next to us for weeks.

My husband, Cricket, came out and we all looked around. And lo and behold, there was the calf in our driveway. It seems the calf had turned at the end of the State Farm fence and come up through the woods to our driveway.

The calf was moseying around a portion of our driveway that is bordered by pasture fence on one side and State Farm fence on the other. All we had to do was close off the driveway at each end and the calf would be penned and then easily caught. It seemed so simple at the time.

First, the fellow who had come to the house drove through our pasture and out the gate to get some help. He returned with several members of the Johnson clan in several pickup trucks. They parked two of them end-to-end across the mouth of the driveway, and they drove two more through the pasture and around to the top of the driveway.

The calf, meanwhile, was getting a tad suspicious of the truck convention and he started looked for an exit through the automotive fences. Various Johnsons ran around waving their arms to shoo him away from the trucks, adding greatly to the calf's interest in being somewhere else.

When the calf was thoroughly suspicious of each and every one of the men and his eyes showed sufficient white around the rims, the Johnsons decided the time was ripe to try to catch him.

Cricket and I sat on the fence and watched with great interest as the cowboys attempted to lasso the calf with a 15-foot section of anchor chain that weighed only slightly less than the calf.

Each man took his turn, climbing off the safety of the pickup-truck fence and arming himself with the anchor chain. The designated roper would circle the calf at what he judged to be a safe distance, which was beyond the calf's established charge range, but which also happened to be beyond the range of the chain lasso.

Periodically, the calf would make a bolt for freedom through a gap that he saw behind the designated roper, and the designated roper would abandon the chain lasso and scramble up on the hood of a pickup truck amid hoots of laughter from the other calf-ropers. Then somebody would toll the calf away from the chain lasso, the designated roper would retrieve it and begin circling the calf again.

Occasionally, one of the men would actually cast the chain lasso in the direction of the calf's head. Fortunately, the calf was quite adept at eluding the lasso, because there would have been 500 pounds of assorted cuts of meat in our driveway if the chain had actually landed on the calf's head.

After some period of time, during which the calf had gotten progressively less interested in the game and more interested in being somewhere else, it occurred to the calf ropers to gang up on the calf. Abandoning the chain and encircling the calf, the calf ropers encouraged each other for one moment of bravery and lunged at the calf.

Five or six men grabbed legs and tails and heads and dragged the unhappy calf to the back of a stake-sided pickup truck. With a mighty heave, they lifted the calf almost up to the level of the truck bed and rolled him over in a heap.

Amid lots of cheerful waving, David Johnson departed with his calf safely imprisoned in the truck.

David Johnson recently had another opportunity to use his livestock penning skills. Two of our horses decided to open the gate and take a stroll to "Contention," a nearby farmette where David works. The colt was easy to catch but the mare was wild. First, David cornered her between the fences lining the driveway.

Then the mare, sensing that this was a man who employed chain lassos, allowed herself to be caught.

CHAPTER 44

Making a Grand Entrance

I n the family lore there is a story illustrating my inborn competitive drive. It seems the three of us children were being called upon to perform in some manner before our aunts and uncles, and I was being disruptive during my brother's performance.

"What is the matter with you?" one of the adults demanded.

"I want to be the frontest," I pouted.

Nearly everybody wants to be the frontest at some time in his life, and nearly everybody has some talent or gift that enables him to be, if only in an humble or fleeting way, the frontest.

My parents will laugh when they read this, but my competitive drive has mellowed a bit with age. After years of experience, I've learned that there is always someone who can do things better. I can outdo some people at some things, but there's always someone who can outdo me, so I don't get too set up about my little victories.

But when I was coming along, I was competitive about everything. At one point in my life I played a lot of tennis, and I took great pleasure one day in winning four games from a fellow who bet I couldn't win but three. I do love a bet.

It's a wonder any boy ever asked me for the second date because I loved outdoing my beaux. My date would drive up in the driveway and Daddy would say, "Now Robin, don't arm wrestle with the poor boy. Or at least let him win."

When I was in the fifth grade, I got into a contest with Billy Tilson to see who could read the most books that year. I won, but the only book I remember reading was a biography of Knute Rockne.

It's dawned on me over the years that being the frontest is frequently a hollow title. I've found my energy and time can often be better spent pursuing goals other than frontestness.

Of course, sometimes being the frontest comes naturally. This is the case with me and my chief talent. When the conversation turns to one-upsmanship, I listen smugly as others recount their accomplishments, because I know there is no one who can top me at my specialty: throwing up at inopportune moments.

I'm afflicted with an exaggerated susceptibility to motion sickness. Gory movies and frightening incidents don't bother me a bit, but put me in the back seat of a Cadillac being driven over a mountain road by a chain-smoking driver and I'll flash before you can said, "Stop the car!"

The only certain way for me to avoid nausea on any trip of more than 600 yards is for me to drive. I get tired of revealing this handicap and sometimes try to tough it out, but it's no use.

Being prone to motion sickness forces you into embarrassing choices. You're in a caravan of cars on the garden club outing, and half way to Williamsburg you feel that sick-green feeling creeping up your throat. Here you are with all these nicely dressed, dignified people, and you have to ask the driver to hand over the keys to her BMW under the threat of your barfing all over the backseat.

People are always sympathetic, but it's embarrassing nevertheless. After all, carsickness is supposed to be a childhood affliction.

Nothing is sacred in my family and we always laughed about my handicap. Daddy and I worked out a good system on the many family trips. I'd make one announcement early on that I was queasy, then suffer in silence until the "10-second count-down." At that point, I'd say in an ominous voice, "Daddy, stop the car." He'd have 10 seconds to pull over so I could open the door and lean out.

The story I tell to establish my prominence in this field is one referred to within the family as "Robin's Grand Entrance at VMI." My older brother went to Virginia Military Institute and the family frequently drove over the mountain from Lynchburg to Lexington to visit him.

As a 14-year-old aspiring prom-trotter, I loved going to VMI, but I hated the drive over the mountains. I always rode in the front seat, which helped some. One day, there was a cigarette-smoking adult riding in the front seat and I was relegated to the smoke-filled back seat.

Of course I knew every rock and tree along the road, and I exerted enormous will power not to get sick during the 43-mile drive. Two more turns and we'll be off the mountain, I'd tell myself, gritting my teeth. Three more miles to Buena Vista, you can hold out that long. Finally, those yellow walls hove into view.

I had worn some outfit that was appropriately seductive for a 14-year-old, and I had great hopes of driving one of my brother's fellow cadets mad with desire. Unfortunately, by the time the car stopped in front of the barracks, charming a cadet was the furthest thing from my mind.

I staggered out of the car, took a few deep breaths of fresh, still, unsmoky air, and thought if I just lean on the car and be quiet for a few minutes, I'll be all right.

At that moment, my mother noticed the green around my gills and asked in alarm, "Are you all right?"

Clearly I wasn't. I was too weak even to answer. All I wanted to do was get my legs and stomach back, if necessary by throwing up on the grass.

As I weakly protested, Momma grabbed me by the wrist and took off running across the parking lot towards the barracks.

In those days, there was a date parlor with a ladies powder room just inside Marshall Arch. Momma's idea was to whisk me into the powder room, but we didn't get that far. Galloping across the pavement upset the last shred of gastronomic equilibrium I possessed. As Momma flung open the door to the date parlor on a collection of startled cadets and their dates, I threw up.

Fortunately, the next year I was old enough to drive, and I arrived at the barracks to visit Bo and his brother rats with much less fanfare and a lot more social success.

That's really the best story, but even without it, I could top most people. There was the time in my teens that I ducked behind a holly bush and blew my cookies on the way into the church for a wedding.

And the time, also in my teens, I was riding home from another wedding with our minister and his wife, and I had to choose between painting the back seat of their Cadillac and making the chic announcement that I wanted to stop and throw up in the ditch.

I even got sick in the movies one time. My brother and I went to see "The Ra Expedition." It was based on Thor Heyerdaal's book about sailing a reed boat across the Atlantic. The whole movie was filmed on the actual journey. The cameraman would stand on the bow and shoot the stern, then he'd run to the stern and shoot the bow.

Of course the whole screen was waving back and forth, complete with the slosh-slosh, creak-creak of the waves and rigging. Pretty soon I was feeling woozy and I sank down in my seat and closed my eyes. But the sound effects were just as damaging as the visual image.

I made it through the show, but on the way home, as my brother rhapsodized about the movie, I said in an ominous voice, "Bo, stop the car."

He barely made the 10-second count-down.

CHAPTER 45

Wedding Bell Blues

I 've always regretted the fact that none of my weddings was held in an area covered by a weekly newspaper. I enjoy reading the accounts of local weddings in weeklies, mostly because weeklies still accord weddings their proper respect in terms of column inches.

Dailies have pared wedding coverage down to name, rank and serial number -- stark facts presented in a rigid format more suited to an obituary. (Actually, I think they could jazz up their obits, too.) If papers are going to cut betrothed couples off at 25 words, they ought at least to permit the couples to include whatever they think is most interesting about their nuptials.

It seems mighty old-fashioned to demand, for instance, that couples limit themselves to one set of parents each, preferably the natural parents. I think they ought to allow anybody who wants to be part of the event to be included.

In the old days, accounts of weddings covered the festivities in exquisite sartorial and familial detail. Newspaper editors claim they don't have enough space for that kind of coverage anymore. They'd have enough room if they didn't run so many stories on weird food like popcorn parmigiana or tofu (any flavor) that make people want to gag.

I subscribe to a rural newspaper that still reports how many feet of Alençon lace (whatever that is) the bride wore and who poured the punch and who caught the bouquet. It's the most entertaining section of the paper.

My all-time favorite account reported on a wedding in a correctional facility. The reporter, obviously not one to stint the happy couple just because of some legal indiscretion, told us about the bride's lacy bodice and filligreed peplum and continued with a description of the groom's light blue leisure tuxedo.

Every detail was solemnly reported in that organ-recital tone-of-voice reserved for weddings. "The seven-year-old daughter of the bride and groom wore a white dress and carried a blue flower." Fellow inmates "assisted." (I always picture the groom, in manacles and chained to a ball, shuffling down the aisle with a buddy helping him carry the hardware.)

The newspaper mentioned everyone who was even tangentially associated with the nuptials: who designed the cake, who fried the chicken, how many aunts came from Zion Crossroads and Piney River. The paper even told us who wasn't there: "Cousin Elloree Ferstner was greatly missed."

Well, maybe newspapers have to draw the line somewhere.

Even within the rigid format dictated by daily newspapers' self-appointed guardians of taste, brides and grooms have found a way to express themselves. In certain quarters, the wedding announcement is viewed as a golden opportunity to settle old scores and rewrite history.

The happy bride, full of love and joy, will ruthlessly eliminate her mother because mommy dearest made an indiscreet remark about the groom's three previous wives. Likewise the groom, in the full flush of romance, will list his mother's boyfriend, who always let him ride motorcycles and smoke cigarettes, and cut out his father, who is giving the happy couple a $3,000 honeymoon.

If you add engagement announcements, couples have two chances to whip their families into shape. Relatives not mentioned in the engagement announcement can take the hint and mend their ways or forget about sitting in the front pew.

I know of one instance where a bride insisted to the wedding editor that she wanted no mention of her father in the announcement. So it ran that way on Sunday. On Monday, the father called the paper and was told the bride didn't want him in there. "That's funny," he said, "I gave her away."

In addition to rewriting biological history, engaged couples often try to rewrite their marital history. No matter how many times they've been married, brides consider the current wedding the only one that counts. They blithely dispose of all rings, titles and names that would indicate their children ever had a legitimate father.

One of my favorite stories concerns the bride who expected to be rejuvenated. A 40-ish woman handed the wedding editor of a daily paper a completed wedding form and a picture of the bride. The wedding editor looked at the picture, which showed a young version of the 40-ish woman, and assumed it was her daughter. But the photograph looked strangely out-of-date, so the wedding editor asked who it was.

"Oh, it's me," said the woman, adding that the photograph was taken at the time of her first marriage, in 1965 or so. "That's the only picture I have of myself in a wedding dress."

A bride always wants to be "Miss" so-and-so, even when her 19-year-old son and his baby deliver the wedding information to the paper. In this age of multiple marriages, untangling the relationships of the families takes a keen mind and ruthless interrogation by the wedding editor.

It seems to me that staff time would be better spent and readers better served if newspapers would just print the whole story. If the bride and groom want to mention all of the parents -- the natural parents, their previous spouses and their current spouses or live-in companions -- so much the better. It saves the reader from having to reconstruct the marital histories of all the participants.

This is what I had in mind:

BOLLING-BALL

The marriage of Miss Fancy Nancy Gaye D. Vorsey Hava Ball, daughter of Mrs. Dorothy Gaye Dawson Jonas and her second and third husbands, and of the late Mr. Falston Gaye and his widow, who is shacking up with a guy named Bob, to Ernest Lee Bolling, son of Dr. Hugh Bolling, the present Mrs. Hugh Bolling, and Miss Susan Bolling (the previous Mrs. Hugh Bolling) and her boyfriend, Chuck, all of Goochland, took place yesterday at the Bowles Farm polo field to accommodate all the people entitled to sit in the front pew.

Mike Jonas, the bride's stepfather, was the ringmaster. Mrs. Falston Gaye, the bride's stepmother, sang selections by Twisted Sister and Cindi Lauper. Chuck, the groom's mother's boyfriend, was the ring bearer. The bride was attended by her two children from her previous marriages and the two she had in high school. Dr. Bolling was not invited to the ceremony.

After a wedding trip to Mineral, the couple will live with the consequences of this announcement for the rest of their lives.

CHAPTER 46

A Tale of Two Goats

ately when I've ventured as far east as Richmond Country Club, I've noticed Austin Brockenbrough's cattle grazing in that open corner of his property across from the golf course. And every time I see them, I notice a tiny calf which turns out not to be a calf at all but a goat.

And every time I see that goat I wonder: Why do they have a goat?

Why does anybody have a goat? You can't do anything with them and they don't make very affectionate pets. They eat up all your grass and they get out and then you have to chase around the countryside after them. About all they're good for is to prevent children from crossing your property.

I know. We had a couple of goats when I was growing up. It was all my daddy's idea.

My daddy must have had a wonderful childhood, because he was always trying to recreate for his own children the experiences he had as a child. One of his fondest memories (and he has many) is of his goat. He got the goat when he was about 11 or so. Everything that ever happened to my daddy happened to him when he was "about 11 or so" or when he was "oh, a senior in high school, I reckon."

It was an Angora billy goat, "a gre-at big one, with long horns." He had the imaginative name of Billy. Not long after Daddy got the goat, Santa Claus brought him a miniature farm wagon that he, Santa, had ordered from Montgomery Ward. It had a green striped body and red wooden wheels with metal rims.

"My daddy made the harness with a hand awl stitcher. He sewed the leather and everything," Daddy recalled.

Daddy would hitch up the goat and run errands all over town, which, in this case, meant driving two or three blocks in any direction. Daddy became quite skilled at driving his goat wagon. "The goat didn't like to go away from home, so you had to sit there and twist his tail to make him go. But when you turned around to go home, why, there was no problem," Daddy said.

One of his favorite chores was to shell a sack of corn and carry it to the mill to grind for grits. "We had grits on the table every day of my life, like a knife and fork. We called it hominy but it was grits," Daddy said.

Driving goats and grinding grits were entertaining for only so long, and Daddy moved on to other pastimes. "Gabe Aiken, from up near Metz's Crossroads, picked up the goat when I was, oh, a senior in high school, I reckon, and took him up to his place and butchered him." Daddy shook his head at the thought. "That was pretty tough eating."

Armed with these happy memories, Daddy sold Momma on the idea that we children needed a goat. (My daddy is a salesman and my momma is real tolerant.) We lived in town at the time. The street wasn't completely built up at the time, but it was town nevertheless.

One Saturday afternoon, we went out to the country and Daddy bought a goat. It was a Toggenberg milk goat with a beautiful sable coat and gently curving horns. My brother, Bo, wanted a billy goat, and since the goat had horns, he called it Billy. Later, when the goat had kids, we changed her name to Nanny.

True to his childhood memories, Daddy made a harness and built a little two-wheeled cart for Nanny. The cart was designed like a sulky and painted red and yellow. It really was a sharp turn-out and I'm sure Bo was the envy of every child on the street, most of whom had to make do with pedestrian amusements like baseball and Tinker Toys.

Bo hired out himself and his goat cart as entertainment for birthday parties. "That was a real money-making operation," Daddy recalled, "by the time I took off from work and hauled the goat and the cart over to the party.

"It was like the time we got in the game chicken business" -- another re-creation of Daddy's childhood – "Flo would sell a trio -- a cock and two hens -- to somebody in Colorado for $12. Then I'd take off half a day from work and scout around to find a crate to ship them in and pack them up and pay the freight. Flo got the $12 and I was about $50 in the hole."

These little setbacks never prevented Daddy from acquiring more livestock, occasionally by unorthodox means.

One day when Daddy was riding his horse over near Manny Yeatts' cottage, he saw a billy goat tied to the fence eating honeysuckle. Nanny was back home bellowing, so Daddy thought he'd give her a thrill. He put her in the station wagon and drove over to Manny Yeatts'. The billy goat paused in his foraging long enough to fall madly in love for a few minutes.

After the appropriate interval, Nanny produced twin kids, one of which died. The surviving twin was a solid white billy goat, named Freddie, who grew up to be enormously fat and unfriendly and the source of my present enmity toward goats.

Since we had a Toggenberg milk goat who had freshened, Daddy's vision of goat-ownership immediately expanded to include the notion of drinking fresh goat's milk every morning. So he tried to interest Bo, who was about 11 or so, in becoming a goat milker. Bo declined. Lording it over the neighborhood children in his goat chariot was one thing, but extracting milk from the semi-private parts of an uncooperative nanny was another.

Daddy was philosophical in his disappointment. "We tried it for a little bit and then we decided to let Freddie have it all because it was too much trouble."

About that time, Momma and Daddy noticed we were beginning to stand out in the neighborhood, what with all the cats and dogs and horses, not to mention the game chickens and goats, all cohabitating on a city lot, and they sensibly moved to the edge of town.

There we had a 15-acre farmette with board-fenced pasture for the horses. I understand people generally make a sort of dog pen for their goats, but Daddy put barbed wire under the fence around 15 acres and turned the goats out with the horses. It didn't work. They went wherever they wanted to.

Most of the time they were content to stay in the pasture and chase the occasional stray child who ventured into the pasture to catch her pony.

But they must have been lonely for their own kind, because they were always getting out, going through the woods and joining a small herd of cattle that lived nearby. The farmer and my mother eventually became cordial friends, and he would call whenever the goats showed up at his barn. Daddy was always out of town when the goats went visiting, so it fell to Momma to pick them up.

At the time when the goats were making frequent visits to see the cattle, Momma had a pink Ford convertible with a black top. It was a snazzy car. And, with the top down, it was exactly the right size for transporting two goats. Although it was a short way to the farmer's through the woods, it was a long way around by the road and involved driving through some distinctly non-agricultural areas of the city.

The goats didn't mind, though. We would toll them into the back seat with a piece of bread and they would ride home in style with their horned heads hanging out the windows. We rode home hiding our heads under the dashboard.

CHAPTER 47

Young People Are Masters
of Vital Skill: Doing Nothing

I did something on Labor Day that I haven't done in a long time: nothing. Nothing of consequence, that is. It was, if you remember, a gorgeous day for it, a crisp, breezy morning after a rainy night, and then a warm, sunny afternoon.

For some wonderful reason, my responsibilities failed to nag me and I wandered from one thing to the next all day, pausing every 15 minutes or so to think, What a glorious day! I don't much care for summer, especially the kind we've been having lately, and every September that first fall-type day when the humidity drops out makes me feel alive again for the first time in months.

Labor Day was such a day. But instead of energizing me to catch up on chores I had fretted about in the heat, the weather simply removed my anxiety about getting the chores done. It was a day to enjoy for itself, one of those rare days when goals and efficiency and tomorrow are put aside in favor of savoring the present.

Most of the day I spent on the living room rug with our nearly year-old daughter, stacking blocks, playing peek-a-boo and generally wallowing around tickling and hugging and kissing. We played some in the yard, too. The minutes rolled by uncounted for a change, as I sat and watched her push the stroller around the grass on her tiptoes or laughed as she squealed and chased the cat on her hands and knees.

When the baby took a nap, I browsed through catalogs from which I never intend to order anything. Later, when a friend appeared to ride one of the horses, I spontaneously joined her. Cricket took over tickling the baby and I took an unscheduled trail ride without worrying about the meter running on a babysitter. I didn't worry about training the horse, either. When he wanted to gallop and buck and play, I laughed and let him.

Doing nothing is a marvelously rewarding way to spend a day or an afternoon because it recharges your brain cells in a way that sleep, vacations and hobbies don't.

The key to doing nothing is aimlessness. You can't go out for a round of golf and call that doing nothing. Playing golf or tennis or going to a horse show requires effort. It involves competition and it involves keeping some schedule -- none of which can be considered doing nothing.

Playing tennis might be fun and relaxing and a good change of pace, but it's not the same as doing nothing. Neither is sightseeing on a vacation, or anything that means checking your watch. Even if your schedule involves going to a party, it's still a schedule. People doing nothing don't have a schedule.

On the other hand, lying on the couch watching television isn't doing nothing, either. Watching television is a terminal activity. Doing nothing involves drifting around mentally and sometimes physically, too, neither of which is possible in front of the boob tube.

Doing nothing is normally considered an activity of youth because youth are the only people who have time to do nothing. They are good at it because they do a lot of it. Ask the next teenager you see what he did over the weekend. I'll bet you a dollar to a doughnut he says, in a voice tinged with surprise, "Nothing."

That doesn't mean he vegetated with the VCR. He got together with some friends and they roamed around, pausing at each other's houses to mull over such imponderables as where to get the best pizza and whether the Redskins will regret trading Jay Schroeder to the Raiders.

Doing nothing isn't the prerogative solely of the young, although it helps to be as untrammeled by responsibility as they are. In these days when both parents work and every member of the household belongs to two clubs and plays three sports, it's nearly impossible to find a half day of down time to do nothing. And yet it's critical to our peace of mind to have those occasional periods of irresponsibility.

I, for one, frequently long for the luxury of an afternoon with no more responsibility than to watch the leaves turn or listen to the doves in the field. Sometimes losing track of time for even half an hour helps.

This is the time of year spiders are spinning webs everywhere. I'm always fascinated by the ones I call "zipper spiders" for the design of their webs. The other day I spent perhaps 20 minutes watching a zipper spider mummify a victim, carry it to the pantry side of its web and then repair the torn web. When I came to and went about my chores, I felt as refreshed as if I'd had a nap.

Watching wildlife isn't the only thing I do when I do nothing. Sometimes I indulge myself with a chore that is so far down the priority list that it could wait for my heirs to do it. We have books stuck around everywhere, on shelves, in boxes, in the attic, on tables. They are fine where they are. Viewed objectively, there are many more tasks that need doing besides sorting our books.

But I love handling books, and I've spent many hours fiddling with my books, doing nothing of consequence, nothing but allowing myself a modest pleasure.

We all need a day left unaccounted for. Not a day of wasted time or a day of structured play, not a day with accomplishments to look back on or even memories to recall, just a day of dreams, a day of modest pleasures.

Lately it seems children's lives are becoming as scheduled as adults' lives, which I find disturbing. My parents must have recognized the importance of free time for children, because in between scout meetings and music lessons and football practice, they saw that we had unhurried time to muse on our own.

When I was young and had a beautiful day before me, I often went outside with a notebook and a box of pens or pastels. I never produced the first sketch, probably because I haven't a lick of artist talent, but I knew there was something fine about such a day that I wanted to capture.

Sometimes I wrote "Chapter One" at the top of a page and dreamed of World Famous Novels I would write. It wasn't a time of seriously developing outlines and plots, just a time for my mind to wander without purpose. Nothing memorable or concrete ever came out of those days, which is the way it should be.

The value of doing nothing is that it gets the gum out of the works, cleans the static off the heads and clears some new disk space for the compositions and calculations of daily life. The day after Labor Day I wrote two articles, schooled my horse and made all sorts of executive decisions about the addition to the house.

Nowadays, when I get an afternoon free of responsibility, I know what to do with it. How terrible it would be if I couldn't remember from childhood how precious and pleasant unstructured play is. Without all those childhood years of practicing doing nothing, I'd never know how, now that it's really important.

O Tannenbaum

I am getting more like my mother every day. Ordinarily, that would be cause for rejoicing, because my mother is admired for many things: her beauty, her charm, her astuteness, her energy. But those are not the areas in which I'm getting more like her.

No, I'm getting more like my mother in her inability to handle everyday chores, chores such as opening a carton of milk without using a fork, finding something to wear that doesn't have cat hair on it, applying paint without leaving brush marks and putting up a really good-looking Christmas tree.

When we children were children, the family always made a thing out of putting up the Christmas tree. Choosing and cutting the tree was almost as big a deal as decorating it. We lived in the country and cut a cedar out of our own woods each year. The children actually did the decorating and, when we were small, there were no ornaments above knee level. I don't remember what any of those trees looked like, but I'm sure they had the beauty that automatically attaches to any project done by a loving family.

When we grew up, though, and blew into the house for Christmas at the last minute, Momma began doing the tree herself. She has always wanted a really terrific-looking, interior-decorator, department-store-window Christmas tree. She has talked about doing a theme tree, where every ornament is a wooden soldier or a dove or a bell or something. And she has talked about a tree all in white or all in red. She even threw out all our old mismatched glass balls with "frost" around the crowns (which are now back in style) and bought a bagful of doves and angels. But somehow she has never quite pulled it off.

Part of it undoubtedly has to do with the trees themselves. My parents moved into town and had to start buying their trees from lots. One year, Daddy must have bought the last tree in Lynchburg. I think it was left over from the year before. You know how trees always have a hole that you put next to the wall? This tree was nothing but holes. It looked like that burnt-out twig Charlie Brown always ends up with. It really was pitiful.

I remember feeling very superior, like I could do better. Pride goeth before a fall.

When Cricket and I got married, I got very excited about putting up our first Christmas tree. Remembering my childhood, I kept thinking about the tradition we were starting. The first two Christmases, a neighbor left fine cedars that he had cut off his farm on our porch. Decorated, they had the beauty that automatically attaches to any project done by a loving family.

Then the third year we decided to get our own. We have some woods near the barn, but of course there isn't a single evergreen on our side of the fence. Just across the fence on our neighbor's land, however, it looks like Santa's own Christmas tree forest. I wanted to ask our neighbor if we could cut one of her cedars, but Cricket said no, he'd pick up a tree at the Jaycee lot. Having grown up in the country when cutting your own tree was half the fun, I couldn't deal with the idea of buying a Christmas tree. Cricket had grown up in town and it seemed like a perfectly sensible idea to him. We argued about it until all the good trees were gone and we ended up with a burnt-out twig like Charlie Brown.

The next year we went to a tree farm and cut one. That made me feel a little better, but I still flinched at the idea of paying so much money for a Christmas tree. I should add here that I also flinch at the idea of a custom that requires the sacrifice of thousands of living trees for the celebration of a religious holiday. I feel very sad when I drive past the Christmas tree lots on Dec. 26 and see all the trees that got cut down and didn't even get used.

It was perfectly natural, then, when I decided last year to get a live, as in potted, Christmas tree. The weather was very mild and it seemed likely that the tree could withstand the shock of being indoors for a week or so before being planted outside. Plus, I had a spot inside the pasture fence where a white pine would look good. Never have I had a worse idea.

I found a lovely tree (on sale, too!) about a week before Christmas and brought it home. I also stopped and bought a giant plastic pot to put it in. Cricket was away and the tree was too heavy for me to unload, so I rode around in the pickup truck with the tree for a couple of days. Finally, he came home and unloaded it and left it in the driveway for a few more days.

On Dec. 22, just as we were getting ready to go to a party, I suggested we bring the tree in the house (another bad idea). In the meantime, it had rained and the root ball was wet, so the tree weighed about 350 pounds. We got a hand truck, loaded the tree and hauled it into the living room. I produced the plastic pot and we prepared to put the tree in it. We both grabbed the trunk, gave a mighty heave and lifted the tree into the pot.

It almost fit.

We sat there sweating and wondering how to make it fit. We turned it around. We tried rearranging the dirt in the burlap bag. It was packed tightly, so we undid the bag, taking care that no more than 80 percent of the dirt spilled all over the living room rug. Pretty soon we had a bare-root tree that still wouldn't go in the pot because one of the roots was too long. Cricket wanted to cut it off, but I said no, you'll kill the tree (as if it had any hope anyway). The only choice at that point was to go on and plant the tree.

So Cricket went out to the pasture and dug a big hole while I tried to scoop up the dirt from the rug. By then, of course, it was 15 minutes before the party started. We got the tree in the ground, mulched and watered it, and ran upstairs to get dressed. We were only an hour late, and besides, we had a beautiful Christmas tree in the pasture.

Christmas Eve we still didn't have a tree in the house, so while Cricket was working on the barn roof, I climbed the fence and cut the top out of a nice cedar on our neighbor's land. We put it up in the living room and there it stayed, beautifully bare, until we had a free evening a day or two after Christmas.

We did finally get some decorations on it, and I guess it looked good because we left it up until the first of February. And even then, the housekeeper was the one who got tired of it and took it down.

So here it is well into December and we're arguing about the Christmas tree again. I wanted to dig up the first one, the one we planted in the pasture, but it had died.

Maybe this is the year we go artificial.

CHAPTER 49

'I See' Said the Blind Man as He Picked up His Hammer and Saw

There are two kinds of men in the world, and I've been married to both. There are the men who are absolutely helpless around the house, and there are men for whom every household chore and repair job is a challenge.

My previous husband was in the first category. His name was Sam. I used to refer to him as "my ex," but such is my diction that people thought his name was "Max."

Max could not, as they say, change a light bulb. I grew up in a family with a father and two brothers who could fix, build, assemble or jury-rig anything. Consequently, I thought all men were like that. So it was with growing amazement and dismay that I realized the man I had married was missing the fixit gene.

It was awesome to realize I faced a lifetime of stuck windows, off-center picture hooks, plumbing emergencies, automobile towing charges and bills for hired craftsmen.

Prior to my marriage to this man, I had never seen a repairman in my life. Actually, for far too long after my marriage, I never saw a repairman, either, because not only did I fail to recognize my husband's incompetence at handyman jobs, he did, too. Both of us believed the old stereotypes about men: that men are mechanical, men can fix things, men have and know how to use tools, etc.

The fact that his idea of "tools" was a fingernail file or the heel of his shoe should have tipped me off.

Having a husband who can't fix things isn't necessarily fatal to a marriage, any more than having a wife who can't cook is. Repairmen, restaurants and Stouffer's were invented just for those marriages.

And there is a certain freedom that comes with a helpless husband. When something needs fixing, you don't have to wait until it gets to the top of your husband's "honey-do" list, you just call a repairman or handyman. Plus, your husband is always free on the weekends to keep the children or go play with you because he is untrammeled by household chores.

On the other hand, helpless husbands have to make a lot of money, because it's expensive to call in craftsmen, tradesmen and handymen all the time. And having a helpless husband pretty much precludes living in the country and certainly eliminates having horses, unless you board them with somebody else. Even if you're a handywoman yourself, it takes two adults and several teenaged slaves to keep even a small country place going.

After all, who can afford to hire someone to bush hog, build jumps, put in a new mulch bed, stack hay, mow, trim, take down that dead tree, build new doors for the hayloft, put a new roof on the workshop, re-hang the gate, fix the steps to the back stoop, disc the garden, put up the purple martin hotel, move the clothes line, rewire the stable, run a new water line to the back field and build a dog pen?

Or how about replacing the leaky kitchen faucet, replacing the faulty light switch, plastering the crack in the ceiling where the shower leaked, hooking up the stereo/TV/VCR or splicing the hose where the dog chewed it in two?

With a list like that, it's easy to see why families with fixit husbands never take vacations or even go to the movies. On the rare occasions when a fixit husband is tired of doing chores around home, he relaxes by repairing the screen doors and furnaces of his friends who are helpless.

Wives of fixit husbands are suckered into thinking their husbands are garnering a lot of IOUs by doing these favors, but the favors are never returned in kind because...remember?...the friends are helpless to begin with.

No matter how long the list gets and how short the time, fixit husbands refuse to hire anyone to do a few of the projects. Their motto is: "Oh, I can do that."

We are putting a two-story addition with a new kitchen and bathroom on our house, and it is killing Cricket to pay a contractor to do it. He comes home every evening, surveys the day's work and says, "Oh, I can do that."

Fixit husbands don't understand that their wives want certain jobs done before the turn of the century.

Fixit husbands and their wives often have different priorities about the chores to be done. The wife may feel it's important to fix the leaking water line or get the dead boat out of the garage where it has moldered for six years. But these obvious emergencies may easily be at the bottom of her husband's list.

We had the house painted in 1984. The shutters needed some repair work before they could be stripped and painted, but because my husband can fix anything, we didn't buy new shutters or get a carpenter to fix the old ones. Cricket put them in the garage and began working on them. He got as far as cutting out squares of wood to reinforce the corners.

No amount of gentle coaxing from me has gotten him to finish fixing the shutters.

It took me awhile, but I finally figured out why the shutters have never risen to the top of Cricket's to-do list: Fixing the shutters doesn't require using any saws.

Cricket's weakness is saws. He has every saw and cutting tool known to man. He has a radial arm saw, a circular saw, a saber saw, a chain saw, a hand saw, a coping saw, a hacksaw, a bow saw and a backsaw in a miter box.

If you count cutting tools, he has a gas-powered weed whacker, a push mower, a riding mower, a bush hog, an electric drill, a tree limb lopper, lopping shears, hedge clippers and rose snippers.

Not all fixit husbands are hung up on saws, but they do prioritize their chores according to which tools they will get to use. The chores at the top of the list will always be those requiring the use of electricity or an internal combustion engine.

As proof, consider this: Recently, Cricket spent all of a gorgeous 70-degree Sunday building, of all things, jumps for my horse. That was infinitely more attractive than finishing the shutters, a job requiring only a hammer and nails, because it required him to make two trips to town and use all his saws on the same day.

The only chore having higher priority than that would be one giving him the excuse to buy a tool he doesn't have.

All these tools breed more tools. Take the tractor, for instance. Cricket bought a tractor and bush hog when our pasture acreage approached double digits, so we could save the $80 or so it cost to hire someone to bush hog. The tractor came with a front-end loader, which we both agree is about the most valuable tool we have, next to the chain saw.

The tractor also came with something called a PTO, power take-off, which runs implements like the bush hog. So when Cricket saw what he was saving on bush hogging, he decided to save more money and buy a giant seed broadcaster, which runs off the PTO, to spread seed and fertilizer on the pasture. Pretty soon he decided to save some more and buy a rake. By then he had saved enough to buy a manure spreader, which in turn saved him enough to buy an auger.

The auger isn't going to save him any money, though, because he's got to buy fence posts for all those holes he's going to dig. On the other hand, he will get to use his chain saw to cut off the tops of the posts.

CHAPTER 50

I Scream, You Scream, We All Scream for Ice Cream

I used to be very scornful of people who ate vanilla ice cream. Vanilla was such a flavorless flavor, and people who preferred vanilla were equally flavorless, my thinking went. I didn't go so far as to categorize vanilla ice creamers as pinko commie fags, but ordering a vanilla cone immediately put people on my list of suspicious personalities.

I was so disillusioned when a friend I had formerly considered to be bright and personable stepped up to the counter one day and said those fatal words, "I'll have a vanilla cone."

It was all right to order vanilla ice cream if you also got chocolate fudge sauce, nuts and whipped cream on top, but a plain old vanilla ice cream cone...? What a waste of an opportunity to eat something fabulous. And anybody who would waste any opportunity to live life to the fullest, even in so small a thing as eating an ice cream cone, obviously had a defective personality.

But lately I've been rethinking my position on vanilla ice cream.

Ice cream is the nectar of the gods and I approach every ice cream-eating opportunity with relish. Chocolate relish, if possible. Ice cream (indeed, desserts in general) ain't ice cream without chocolate, be it chips, sauce, sprinkles or swirls.

Nuts run a close second to chocolate as an indispensable flavoring of ice cream.

My all-time favorite concoction involving ice cream is a sugar cone with a scoop of mint chocolate chip on the bottom and a scoop of maple walnut on the top. The year I was expecting, I had a bowl of Haagen-Daas' chocolate chocolate chip five nights a week and rum raisin two nights.

Then I gave birth to a child with extraordinary quantities of personality.

My daddy loves ice cream about as much as anybody I know. Now there's a person with personality. You'd never catch him doing something bland like eating a vanilla ice cream cone! In fact, he likes such exotic combinations of flavors that he is embarrassed to order them. At least, he used to be.

When I was coming along, my daddy and I spent a lot of time wandering around together. Mostly he took me to horse shows, but I remember traveling around with him without the horse trailer some, too. And every time we took a trip together, at some point during the day, Daddy would say, "I know a gooooood place right up here to get ice cream. What do you say we stop and get a cone?"

It used to be that chocolate chip was about the most exotic flavor you could get. You had vanilla (for all the colorless people out there), chocolate (for the people with personality) and strawberry (for the people with personality who had some defective gene in them that made them dislike chocolate).

High's and Howard Johnson's were the only places which had other flavors, and most of those had fruit in them, which meant they were just variations on strawberry when it came to judging the personality of the customer. Daddy used to know the location of every High's in the state of Virginia and also most of Maryland and North Carolina.

So we'd stop and Daddy would pull out his wallet and give me a five or a ten. This was in the days when ice cream cones were 29 cents for one scoop, 39 cents for two and no sales tax added. And he'd send me into the store alone to buy two ice cream cones.

Now that the world has been graced with Baskin-Robbins, Friendly's, Haagen-Daas, Glasden Fruje and a whole host of gourmet ice cream parlors with unpronounceable names, it is socially acceptable for a grown man to eat any flavor or color of ice cream he chooses. But 50 years ago, my daddy had the uncomfortable feeling that it was not befitting his position as head of the household to eat a triple-decker cone of butter pecan, pistachio and cherry garden.

Eventually, social attitudes caught up with his progressive position on ice cream, but now he has the uncomfortable feeling that it is not befitting his waistline to eat a triple-decker cone of whatever outlandish flavors.

I'm having a small crisis of attitude regarding preferences in ice cream myself.

As incredible as it sounds, lately I have been eating vanilla ice cream with distressing regularity. Let me hasten to assure you that I always put fresh, sliced peaches, or chocolate chips and pecans, or a jigger of amaretto on my ice cream, but I confess I do start with vanilla. I haven't stooped to eating a vanilla cone, of course, nor do I expect to.

It is inconceivable, of course, that I have developed a vanilla personality (although having a baby does strange things to you). It can't be me, so it must be the ice cream.

One thing I've discovered recently is that vanilla is actually a flavor, rather than the absence of flavor. My husband, Cricket, helped me to that discovery.

Cricket says you have to pay for quality in ice cream. There's no such thing as good, inexpensive ice cream, he says. So I've been forking out huge sums of money for what amounts to a coffee mug of ice cream, and I've found that really good quality vanilla ice cream has some flavor. Not that it can't be improved upon with nuts and chocolate chips, but it does have some flavor of its own.

Lisa Watt, who roomed with me one summer during my tour of the colleges and universities of Virginia and who has personality coming out of her ears, began all sorts of recipes with vanilla ice cream. "Vanilla ice cream," she would say as she whipped up an ice cream and cheese souffle, "is the divine medium."

She had the kind of inflection that put an "h" in divine: "di-vhine." Of course, when she wasn't in the mood for ice cream, she thought bourbon was the divine medium.

Lisa and I often walked to the Howard Johnson's near our apartment and got ice cream cones of various wonderful flavors. Since it was summer, we usually ended up wearing our ice cream before we got to the end of our cones.

I still have that problem. Not only do I flick little flecks of ice cream onto my shirt with every lick, sometimes I push the whole top scoop off in my lap, or in my other hand if I'm standing up and my reflexes are good.

At such times, I'm reminded of a wonderful cartoon that used to be on my refrigerator door. It showed an ice cream vendor leaning over the counter to hand a cone to a wide-eyed little boy. The cone had 14 scoops of ice cream, and the vendor was saying, "Understand: the management takes no responsibility for structural stability."

When Daddy buys a cone, he gets pistachio. When he goes to the store and buys a box of ice cream, he gets butter pecan.

When I buy a cone, I get something with nuts in it. When I go to the store and buy a box of ice cream, I get mint chip.

I called Cricket and asked him what flavor of ice cream he got when he bought a cone. "Chocolate," he said.

"All right," I continued, "when you go to the grocery store and buy a box of ice cream, what flavor do you get?"

"I don't go to the grocery store. You go to the grocery store," he said.

And lately, I buy vanilla.

CHAPTER 51

Christmas Toys
Bring Christmas Joys

So that's what it's like to be a parent at Christmas: 10,000 little pieces of colored plastic all over the family room floor and a toddler playing with the wrapping paper.

Being a parent at Christmas was another learning experience for Cricket and me.

We were, of course, parents last Christmas, parents of a cooing blob in a bucket, a three-month-old baby whose contribution to the Christmas confusion was to smile indulgently as we propped her up in ridiculous poses for the camera. But this year we had a walking, talking ("kitty," "yight," "shoe") toy-consumer whom we were delighted to shower with plastic expressions of our adoration.

Early in December, I spent several afternoons studying the offerings of various toy vendors. Thanks to my niece and nephew, Sarah, 9, and Joe, 7, I had some familiarity with contemporary toys. I'd seen Sarah's 127 different Barbie dolls in all their tawdry, soft-porn splendor. From Joe I had learned about Castle Greyskull and Go-bots.

Nevertheless, I was stunned by the variety of toys available, as well as the assumption that consumers knew what they were. For instance, I gathered from posters and advertisements that something called "Nintendo" was the gift of the year. I thought it was a kung-fu movie, probably the sequel to "Return of the Ninja." Only later did I learn, from Sarah and Joe, that it was a series of sophisticated video games.

Next, I was dismayed by the junky aspect of most of the toys. Everything is plastic, of course, and appears ready to self-destruct the moment it is touched by a child's hand. (This theory was borne out in practice on

Christmas morning.)

Plus, every item, including some of the books, requires batteries.

Also, every item costs either $8.99 or $70. There is nothing in between. Blocks, books, Pla-Doh, action figures (euphemism for dolls for boys), trucks and simple games cost $8.99. Molded plastic tree houses, electronic dolls and their paraphernalia, computers with built-in games and snow sleds cost $70.

Despite all this, I had the urge to buy every toy Katherine Bolling could ever ask for over the next 10 years. I had to restrain myself from buying her a chemistry set, for instance, and a pink bicycle with plastic fringe hanging out of the handlebars.

It dawned on me that, contrary to its image, Christmas is not for children. Christmas is for parents. The Bible was right: It is more blessed to give than receive, and more fun, too. As Cricket and I watched Katherine Bolling explore her toy car and cobbler's bench, I realized the excitement my momma and daddy must have felt those years when one of us children received a really special present.

Momma and Daddy, I now realize, hunted up great gifts just so they could see the excitement on our faces when we opened them. I'm sure they got their money's worth out of me in 1959, when Santa Claus brought me a pony.

Likewise, my older brother, Bo, thrilled them with his excitement over a Lionel train one year and a black-and-tan coonhound another year.

But the apex of gift-giving excitement for my parents must have come in 1965, when Santa brought my younger brother a go-cart. Cris was almost incoherent with joy at the sight of the machine, which Santa had thoughtfully parked in the hall at the foot of the stairs.

Cris had the flu and couldn't go outside, so Santa, ever indulgent, let Cris fire up the go-cart in the hall and drive it (slowly) around the house.

This year, Cricket and I anticipated similar shrieks of joy from our baby daughter. In fact, we got so excited over Katherine Bolling's gifts that we wouldn't let her play with them. She would rip the paper off a package and one of us would help her open the box. Then she would drag, say, a tractor out of the box and lay it on its side, where she would amuse herself by spinning the big rear wheel.

We knew, of course, that you were supposed to set a tractor on its wheels, push it around and say "rudden, rudden." We tolerated Bolling's misuse of her tractor for two or three minutes before we pushed it aside and helped her rip the paper off another package.

That package contained a jack-in-the-box, which we helped her crank two or three times to the tune of Pop Goes the Weasel. She was amused but not overcome with mirth, so we took that toy away and made her open another one. What she wanted to do, and what she did later when her parents finally left her alone, was to figure out how to put the jack back in the box and close the lid.

In the meantime, though, we made her open her xylophone and showed her how to hold the baton and bong the tone bars. She loved the xylophone, but her idea of playing with the instrument was to throw the tone bars on the brick floor, where they made a sound like glass shattering.

What Cricket and I had tried to do was give Katherine Bolling semi-educational toys, things that required her involvement in some way. But as it happens, a child turns everything to his own ends, so it doesn't matter what you give him. Having exhausted the intellectual challenge of a jack-in-the-box in roughly 12 minutes, Katherine Bolling turned to the more imaginative possibilities found in crinkled wrapping paper.

I wouldn't say Christmas was a bust, but I've seen that child more excited about a bowl of oatmeal than she was about her new toys.

At first, Cricket and I attributed her casual attitude to her extreme youth. But a few days later, we visited Betty Allen Graham, the mother of two boys, eight and six, and saw what it takes to make a child's face light up on Christmas.

Betty Allen's boys dazzled Katherine Bolling with their little cars zizzing around tracks with loop-de-loops, an 18-wheel motorized caterpillar that crawled over legs and up stairs, and an electronic game board with lights, bells and whistles.

So much for educational toys and toys that are "appropriate" for 15-month-old girls. I'm going to Radio Shack tomorrow and have another go at this Santa thing.

I wonder if our hall is wide enough for a go-cart?

CHAPTER 52

Biomedical Breakthrough in Goochland

(GOOCHLAND, VA-APRIL 1) Goochland has a rare strain of squirrel that is creating quite a stir among biologists, medical researchers and county officials. Discovered by Dr. Miguel Caracas, a visiting biochemist at J. Sargeant Reynolds Community College, Western Branch, the unusual subspecies is called Scuiridae Vulpes Goochlandae. SVG looks very much like its relative, the fox squirrel, but it is larger and has more of a gray color than the ruddy fox squirrel.

The large, gray Goochla nd squirrels are concentrated around the Courthouse, although a few have been seen in Boscobel and along the seventh hole at Hermitage Country Club.

Dr. Caracas began studying local squirrels after he noticed their rejection of natural food --acorns and berries --in favor of junk food. "We walked through your courthouse lawn in September and the squirrels were feeding on the potato chips and Twinkies construction workers gave them."

Although he offered the squirrels holly berries and generic nuts, their normal food, they were not interested. Intrigued, he trapped a squirrel and began analyzing its body chemistry.

After spending the winter in the laboratory comparing local squirrels with other varieties, Dr. Caracas made the announcement this week about the new subspecies.

"It is my belief that Vulpes Goochlandae is a mutant variety that has interbred and developed into a viable subspecies. The heavy diet of fat and sugar has stimulated overproduction of the enzyme elactimyne. This has produced the characteristic color and unusual size of Vulpes

Goochlandae."

"The development of a new species is an encouraging sign at a time when some species of plant or animal becomes extinct every week," said Louisa Ferncliff, a spokesman for FLAG (For the Love of Animals in Goochland).

On Friday, the Board of Supervisors issued a proclamation urging citizens to feed local squirrels peanuts, potato chips and Twinkies. Sunday, normally a quiet day around the Courthouse, hundreds of people came to the square and dumped cupcakes and potato chips all over the lawn.

When Deputy Joe Smith tried to stop one woman from littering, she threw peanut shells in the officer's face and stuck a copy of the proclamation to his badge with chewing gum. The woman, who was not identified, was arrested and led away shouting, "Nuts to the squirrels!"

Medical researchers think the Goochland squirrels could make a significant contribution to medicine. An enzyme that is structurally similar to elactimyne but which occurs only in an endangered species of wharf rat has shown promise as an antidote to old age. Scientists are hopeful that elactimyne could be substituted.

Dr. Caracas is teaming with the Goochland Historical Society to hold a conference on the squirrels in connection with Goochland County Day. Biologists and tourists from Sweden, West Germany and Sandy Hook have already expressed an interest in coming to the conference, tentatively titled, "Goochland Squirrels: From Revolutionary War to Revolutionary Medicine".

In addition to medical lectures, there will be a program outlining the influence of Goochland squirrels on Williamsburg architecture and a slide show covering famous squirrels of the Civil War period.

As a preliminary to the international conference, researchers are planning to trap hundreds of the squirrels for further research. The announcement on Thursday of the squirrel hunt brought an outcry from game warden E. Byrd Johnson.

"Squirrels are out of season until September," said Johnson. "I don't care if they can cure nuclear fallout, trapping squirrels at this time is against the law." Johnson said agents of the Game and Inland Fisheries Commission would "do whatever's necessary" to protect the squirrels.

Late last night, 16 agents of the Game Commission were camped around the statue on the Courthouse lawn. They are taking turns manning howitzers at the entrances to the square. Sheriff Amos's men are also working double shifts to provide secondary manpower.

Most of the agents said they were willing to die to protect the squirrels.

"If the squirrels here are so great, what do they want to kill them for? It must be some kinda Commie plot," said Bubba Cantwell, who wore combat gear and was armed with an M-16 rifle.

Mrs. Ferncliff, when told of the Game Commission's plans, called a press conference to announce that FLAG would initiate an adopt-a-squirrel program to protect the rodents. Kay Higgins of Crozier adopted the first one.

When told of the response to his squirrelly project, Dr. Caracas said, "What is this? Some kind of joke?"

CHAPTER 53

Blessed Be the Ties that Bind

My uncle died this summer. We were all sad, but he had not been well and the time had come. I had not seen him much over the past 12 years, not since I married and had a family, but we had retained a closeness developed over many years of frequent family gatherings.

There comes a time when families gather only for weddings and funerals. Ours is like that now, at least for my generation of the cousins. The last time we were all together, the last time I saw Uncle Riley, was at his granddaughter's wedding three years ago.

Such is the dynamic of the family now that the memories of Elizabeth's wedding and Uncle Riley's funeral are similar. There were late-night conversations in various relatives' motel rooms, convivial reminiscences over spirits at the reception and protracted farewells on the front walk.

There was the appropriate observation of solemnity at each event, but before and after the central ceremony, we celebrated the family.

The wedding ceremony and the funeral rites were touching, moving experiences, as those two events always should be. But they were moving in a way that transcended our feelings for the bride or the deceased. The observation of these two rites fundamental to every family reinforced the feeling of kinship among us.

Some families have this to a greater degree than others. In our family, there is an indescribably intense bond among the kinfolk, even unto the third cousins. During the Gulf War, my daughter and I prayed nightly for the safe return of "Jody's boy." I first met Jody's boy, my third cousin once removed, this summer at Uncle Riley's funeral, more than a year after the war. Yet I worried about him more deeply than I did about a friend who was also in the war.

There was a joyousness in the family gathering after the funeral that would have pleased Uncle Riley, I believe. He had a great sense of family himself, and he had shared the blood-tie bonding at other family funerals and weddings.

Much of that bonding comes from retelling the family lore. We all told our favorite stories about Uncle Riley, stories illustrating his gentle manner, his keen observations and his love of family.

One of my favorites was about Uncle Riley's ladder. He had the longest ladder in the neighborhood, and the neighbors were forever borrowing it to clean their gutters. Once, after the ladder had been passed around for several months, Uncle Riley went looking for it. He found it at the house of a neighbor who was away for several weeks, so he asked the neighbor's gardener for it. The gardener replied stiffly that Uncle Riley would have to ask the owner if he could use the ladder.

Someone else recalled the time Gen. Norman Schwartzkopf's wife came to call. At the time, Uncle Riley could scarcely stand without assistance, but when the general's wife entered the room, gentleman that he was, he rose to his feet

There were many other stories, too, mostly about escapades of the cousins in their youth. We tell these stories every time we get together. You can't remember these things unless you practice remembering them. That's why it's so important, whenever and wherever there is a family wedding or funeral, to go.

Also at Uncle Riley's funeral, we learned that Elizabeth, the bride of three years, was expecting a baby. It was an eminently fitting announcement.

About the Author

Robin Traywick Williams

Robin Williams has more energy and more fun than anybody you know. When she began sharing her humorous view of such topics as modern male chivalry and how to get your spouse to stop smoking, her columns became an immediate hit. She has a wonderful sense of both the ridiculousness and the importance of everyday events.

A graduate of the Hollins University masters writing program, Robin attended many of the colleges and universities of Virginia as an undergraduate. In the 1980s, she was an award-winning reporter for the Richmond Times-Dispatch and followed that with an award-winning stint as editor of a rural weekly newspaper. In 2008, she received the Virginia Writers' Club's Golden Nib Award for a chapter from her novel manuscript, "The Key to the Quarter Pole."

She ran a close second in her first steeplechase and in her first campaign for the Virginia General Assembly, but she came home a winner when she married Charles "Cricket" Williams. They have a grown daughter and a full complement of cats, dogs, horses and, unfortunately, ground hogs.

Robin Williams is President of the Thoroughbred Retirement Foundation. She is also a former chairman of the Virginia (Horse) Racing Commission and served as chief-of-staff for former Lt. Governor John H. Hager. She is a member of the board of directors of Community Bankers Trust Corp.

For more on Robin, see her website: robintraywickwilliams.com.

September 2010